Securing Blockchain Networks like Ethereum and Hyperledger Fabric

Learn advanced security configurations and design principles to safeguard Blockchain networks

Alessandro Parisi

BIRMINGHAM - MUMBAI

Securing Blockchain Networks like Ethereum and Hyperledger Fabric

Commissioning Editor: Sunith Shetty
Acquisition Editor: Srikanth Varanasi
Content Development Editor: Nathanya Dias
Senior Editor: Ayaan Hoda
Technical Editor: Utkarsha S. Kadam
Copy Editor: Safis Editing
Project Coordinator: Aishwarya Mohan
Proofreader: Safis Editing
Indexer: Manju Arasan
Production Designer: Joshua Misquitta

First published: April 2020

Production reference: 1100420

Published by Packt Publishing Ltd.
Livery Place
35 Livery Street
Birmingham
B3 2PB, UK.

ISBN 978-1-83864-648-6

www.packt.com

Packt>

Subscribe to our online digital library for full access to over 7,000 books and videos, as well as industry leading tools to help you plan your personal development and advance your career. For more information, please visit our website.

Why subscribe?

- Spend less time learning and more time coding with practical eBooks and Videos from over 4,000 industry professionals

- Improve your learning with Skill Plans built especially for you

- Get a free eBook or video every month

- Fully searchable for easy access to vital information

- Copy and paste, print, and bookmark content

Did you know that Packt offers eBook versions of every book published, with PDF and ePub files available? You can upgrade to the eBook version at www.packt.com and as a print book customer, you are entitled to a discount on the eBook copy. Get in touch with us at customercare@packtpub.com for more details.

At www.packt.com, you can also read a collection of free technical articles, sign up for a range of free newsletters, and receive exclusive discounts and offers on Packt books and eBooks.

About the author

Alessandro Parisi has been an IT professional for over 20 years, acquiring significant experience as a security data scientist and as an artificial intelligence cybersecurity and blockchain specialist. He has experience of operating within organizational and decisional contexts characterized by high complexity. Over the years, he has helped companies to adopt artificial intelligence and blockchain DLT technologies as strategic tools in protecting sensitive corporate assets. He holds a master's degree in economics and statistics.

To my wife Ilaria, for all her love and patience!

About the reviewers

Samanyu Chopra is a developer, entrepreneur, and blockchain supporter with broad experience in conceptualizing, developing, and producing computer and mobile software. He has been programming since the age of 11. He is proficient in programming languages such as JavaScript, Scala, C#, C++,and Swift. He has a wide range of experience in developing for desktop and mobile. He has been a supporter of Bitcoin and blockchain since their early days and has been part of wide-ranging decentralized projects for a long time. You can connect with him via LinkedIn.

Narendranath Reddy is an experienced full-stack blockchain engineer and Hyperledger Fabric expert with a proven track record of helping enterprises to build production-ready, blockchain-backed applications. He is an experienced innovator and creative thinker. He has won four hackathons on blockchain and is a keynote speaker, regularly speaking about blockchain and distributed ledgers. He is currently working as a blockchain software engineer at ConsenSys, in Dubai, and previously worked as a blockchain developer at Blockgemini in Dubai and as a software developer at UST Global, Trivandrum, and in Spain, Madrid.

Packt is searching for authors like you

If you're interested in becoming an author for Packt, please visit `authors.packtpub.com` and apply today. We have worked with thousands of developers and tech professionals, just like you, to help them share their insight with the global tech community. You can make a general application, apply for a specific hot topic that we are recruiting an author for, or submit your own idea.

Table of Contents

Section 2: Architecting Blockchain Security

Section 3: Securing Decentralized Apps and Smart Contracts

Preface

Blockchain adoption has extended from niche research to everyday usage. However, despite the blockchain revolution, one of the key challenges faced in blockchain development is maintaining security, and this book will demonstrate the techniques for doing this.

You'll start with blockchain basics and explore various blockchain attacks on user wallets, and denial of service and pool mining attacks. Next, you'll learn cryptography concepts, consensus algorithms in blockchain security, and design principles while understanding and deploying security implementation guidelines. You'll not only cover architectural considerations, but also work on system and network security and operational configurations for your Ethereum and Hyperledger Fabric network. You'll later implement security at each level of blockchain app development, understanding how to secure various phases of a blockchain app using an example-based approach. You'll gradually learn to securely implement and develop decentralized apps, and follow deployment best practices. Finally, you'll explore the architectural components of Hyperledger Fabric, and how they can be configured to build secure private blockchain networks.

By the end of this book, you'll have learned blockchain security concepts and techniques that you can implement in real blockchain production environments.

Who this book is for

This book is for blockchain developers, security professionals, and Ethereum and Hyperledger developers who are looking to implement security in blockchain platforms and ensure secure data management using an example-driven approach. Basic knowledge of blockchain concepts will be beneficial.

What this book covers

Chapter 1, *Introducing Blockchain Security and Attack Vectors*, illustrates the core concepts and fundamental elements of blockchain technology, such as distributed ledgers, peer-to-peer network topology, and consensus protocols.

Chapter 2, *Cryptography Essentials*, introduces cryptography primitives and their use in blockchain, looking at the differences between cryptography algorithms and hashing algorithms and how cryptography primitives fit into blockchain architecture.

Chapter 3, *Blockchain Security Assumptions*, focuses on the assumptions made about blockchain security and potential threats related to centralized and decentralized models. We will analyze different types of blockchains and distributed ledger technologies, such as permissioned and permissionless architectures.

Chapter 4, *Trustless Blockchain Networks*, looks at trustless blockchain networks, analyzing how blockchains achieve decentralization by leveraging peer-to-peer networking. We will also see how blockchains manage transactions and show how to protect wallets and private keys.

Chapter 5, *Securing Hyperledger Fabric*, is where we analyze the security aspects relating to Hyperledger Fabric, showing how Hyperledger provides protection against the most common security threats.

Chapter 6, *Decentralized Apps and Smart Contracts*, explores decentralized applications and the core concepts of smart contracts, dealing with central aspects such as developing, creating, and executing decentralized apps and smart contracts in the Ethereum environment.

Chapter 7, *Preventing Threats for DApps and Smart Contracts*, goes into the security aspects of decentralized applications and smart contracts, showing security best practices to prevent potential threats and attacks. We will also learn how to leverage pentesting tools to assess decentralized applications and potential flaws in smart contracts.

Chapter 8, *Exploiting Blockchain as an Attack Vector*, looks into how a blockchain can become an attack vector for data integrity compromises, identity theft, and malware.

Chapter 9, *Analyzing Privacy and GDPR Compliance Issues*, analyzes potential privacy issues for blockchain technology, particularly in terms of EU privacy law (GDPR) compliance.

To get the most out of this book

No particular software or operating system is required to follow the book's content, apart from an up-to-date version of a web browser and an internet connection to download source code examples and the tools suggested in the book. A good understanding of the plaforms such as Hyperledger, Fabric, and Ethereum can be an added advantage. Previous knowledge of blockchain technology would be beneficial, but is not strictly necessary. To get the most out of the book, you are expected to be fluent in networking security core concepts and to have some exposure to a general-purpose programming language.

If you are using the digital version of this book, we advise you to type the code yourself or access the code via the GitHub repository (link available in the next section). Doing so will help you avoid any potential errors related to the copying and pasting of code.

Download the example code files

You can download the example code files for this book from your account at `www.packt.com`. If you purchased this book elsewhere, you can visit `www.packtpub.com/support` and register to have the files emailed directly to you.

You can download the code files by following these steps:

1. Log in or register at `www.packt.com`.
2. Select the **Support** tab.
3. Click on **Code Downloads**.
4. Enter the name of the book in the **Search** box and follow the onscreen instructions.

Once the file is downloaded, please make sure that you unzip or extract the folder using the latest version of:

- WinRAR/7-Zip for Windows
- Zipeg/iZip/UnRarX for Mac
- 7-Zip/PeaZip for Linux

The code bundle for the book is also hosted on GitHub at `https://github.com/PacktPublishing/-Securing-Blockchain-Networks-like-Ethereum-and-Hyperledger-Fabric`. In case there's an update to the code, it will be updated on the existing GitHub repository.

We also have other code bundles from our rich catalog of books and videos available at `https://github.com/PacktPublishing/`. Check them out!

Code in Action

Code in Action videos for this book can be viewed at `https://bit.ly/2xZyAoE`.

Download the color images

We also provide a PDF file that has color images of the screenshots/diagrams used in this book. You can download it here: `https://static.packt-cdn.com/downloads/9781838646486_ColorImages.pdf`.

Conventions used

There are a number of text conventions used throughout this book.

`CodeInText`: Indicates code words in text, database table names, folder names, filenames, file extensions, pathnames, dummy URLs, user input, and Twitter handles. Here is an example: "An example of a Bitcoin address follows: `mwog86wxZsWf6KGufzwA69xbvzE9TGZ5vA`."

A block of code is set as follows:

```
>>> import math
>>> print math.gcd (5, 72)
>>> 1
```

Any command-line input or output is written as follows:

```
bitcoin-cli getnewaddress
```

 Warnings or important notes appear like this.

 Tips and tricks appear like this.

Get in touch

Feedback from our readers is always welcome.

General feedback: If you have questions about any aspect of this book, mention the book title in the subject of your message and email us at `customercare@packtpub.com`.

Errata: Although we have taken every care to ensure the accuracy of our content, mistakes do happen. If you have found a mistake in this book, we would be grateful if you would report this to us. Please visit www.packtpub.com/support/errata, selecting your book, clicking on the Errata Submission Form link, and entering the details.

Piracy: If you come across any illegal copies of our works in any form on the Internet, we would be grateful if you would provide us with the location address or website name. Please contact us at copyright@packt.com with a link to the material.

If you are interested in becoming an author: If there is a topic that you have expertise in and you are interested in either writing or contributing to a book, please visit authors.packtpub.com.

Reviews

Please leave a review. Once you have read and used this book, why not leave a review on the site that you purchased it from? Potential readers can then see and use your unbiased opinion to make purchase decisions, we at Packt can understand what you think about our products, and our authors can see your feedback on their book. Thank you!

For more information about Packt, please visit packt.com.

Section 1: Blockchain Security Core Concepts

1

In this section, you will be introduced to the fundamental primitives of cryptography, along with blockchain's core concepts. With this information under your belt, you will be able to understand the specific design features the blockchains and distributed ledger technology.

This section comprises the following chapters:

- Chapter 1, *Introducing Blockchain Security and Attack Vectors*
- Chapter 2, *Cryptography Essentials*
- Chapter 3, *Blockchain Security Assumptions*

Introducing Blockchain Security and Attack Vectors

1

In this chapter, we will introduce the fundamental constitutive elements of blockchain technology, such as distributed ledger, peer-to-peer network topology, and consensus algorithms, all of which will be further explored in depth in the chapters that follow.

These notions are essential to fully understand the aspects of cyber security associated with blockchain technology, especially with regard to identifying possible attack vectors.

In particular, we will cover the following topics in this chapter:

- An introduction to blockchain
- The building blocks of blockchain
- Blockchain network topology
- Establishing trust through consensus algorithms
- Potential threats that affect trust

An introduction to blockchain

The **blockchain** is often compared to the **internet** in terms of innovation potential. Just as the network of networks has allowed information and ideas to circulate globally, allowing for the reduction of gaps in terms of space and time, in the same way, the blockchain proposes to become the **Internet of Value**.

Another aspect that unites the internet and blockchain is their ability to disintermediate the productive sectors (starting from the financial one) to reduce the areas of inefficiency and allow the emergence of innovative solutions, thereby overcoming the rigidity derived from the status quo preserved by incumbent operators.

Blockchain as the Internet of Value

Blockchain is commonly defined as the Internet of Value in comparison to the traditional internet. To understand the definition of the Internet of Value, let's briefly introduce the limitations of the traditional internet.

Since the first e-commerce experiments that were conducted on the traditional internet, a series of problems have emerged that have to do with the guarantee of authenticity. This involves various factors in the field, such as the following:

- Identity of counterparties in transactions
- Ownership of the rights of the transactions
- Guaranteeing the financial solvency of counterparties

Intermediaries that traditionally guaranteed such factors (typically, banks) have proven to be ineffective in a dematerialized environment such as digital commerce on the internet. The need has, therefore, emerged not only to guarantee users immunity from identity theft, or the holders of copyright from infringement, but also to guarantee the reliability of the means of payment themselves.

By fulfilling this need, the blockchain has become the Internet of Value.

Understanding the emergence of Bitcoin

In coincidence with the financial crisis of 2007-2008, a digital currency, Bitcoin, was introduced for the first time. First and foremost, it was intended to ensure that its value was protected from inflation, without being conditioned by the monetary policies of central banks.

The protection that was provided regarding the value of the currency against erosion caused by inflation, together with its independence from the central monetary authorities, testifies to the aim of introducing a democratic means of payment, which can also act as an alternative (and in competition) currency to the traditional national currencies.

It is no coincidence that many citizens of politically unstable countries have decided to use Bitcoin as a reserve currency, precisely because of the guarantees that this digital instrument provides with respect to the fragility of national currencies.

Like any self-respecting coin, even Bitcoin is based on an essential element that is constituted by trust.

The concept of currency trust translates into practice as follows:

- Conservation of currency value over time
- Protection against possible counterfeiting attempts
- A general acceptance of money as a means of payment

To this end, given the dematerialized nature of Bitcoin, it was necessary to set up a technological infrastructure that would guarantee these prerequisites and be responsible for preserving the trust in transactions between operators.

This technological infrastructure, which is the basis of Bitcoin, is the blockchain.

Blockchain use cases beyond Bitcoin

The blockchain is a technological infrastructure through which it is possible to certify value transactions (which are not limited to the exchange of currencies but can include any type of asset) between trusted counterparties, without the need for the intervention of a central authority (be it banks, government regulators, brokers, and so on).

To perform these tasks, the blockchain is organized into a sequence of blocks (hence the name, *block* and *chain*) that contain the references of the transactions that took place over time. For each transaction that's entered into the blocks, a reference is associated with the previous and subsequent transactions. Finally, the blocks are stored in a shared register (blockchain ledger).

The main feature of the blockchain ledger is that it is append-only; that is, each registration is appended to the pre-existing ones, and the integrity of the ledger is guaranteed by the use of the cryptographic primitives offered by the **Public Key Infrastructure** (**PKI**), which we will cover in more depth in Chapter 2, *Cryptography Essentials*.

The other element that characterizes the blockchain is its network topology, which follows the peer-to-peer protocol. This is used to realize the decentralization of the infrastructure, thereby eliminating the need for a central authority that guarantees the reliability and integrity of transactions.

In practice, a copy of the ledger is saved at each node of the peer-to-peer network; in this way, users taking part in the blockchain can always obtain a copy of the ledger by contacting any of the peer-to-peer network nodes without needing to contact a predefined central node.

Whenever a new transaction is added to the blockchain, all copies of the ledger that are saved within the nodes of the peer to peer network are updated accordingly.

To summarize, the blockchain is characterized by the following elements:

- The presence of a shared ledger within a peer-to-peer network.
- Value transactions are recorded in append-only mode within the ledger.
- The reliability and integrity of the transactions recorded within the ledger is guaranteed by the use of cryptography.

Each new transaction that's entered into the blockchain determines the corresponding update for the ledger and the copies of it present in each node of the peer-to-peer network. In this way, it is possible to do without a central authority that guarantees the reliability and integrity of the transactions that are carried out within the network.

The role played by the distributed ledger

One of the revolutionary ideas of the Bitcoin blockchain was to introduce the distributed ledger mechanism. Satoshi (the pseudonym that the creator of Bitcoin is hidden behind) had, in fact, realized that the main reason for the intervention of intermediaries (in particular, banks) in transactions between private individuals was linked to the management of such transactions. These were recorded in a centralized ledger book. Satoshi's intuition was to replace the centralized ledger, which was managed by the corresponding central authorities, with a shared public ledger that's updated by the same subjects participating in value transactions.

However, with this, a series of problems remained to be solved:

- How to ensure that this shared ledger is tamper-proof and that it is robust with respect to arbitrary changes
- How to guarantee an adequate degree of confidentiality to the subjects who carry out value transactions
- How to properly manage the size of the ledger, since each transaction must be registered in it

To solve these problems, the blockchain was created. Now, let's take a look at the building blocks of blockchain.

The building blocks of blockchain

Now, we're going to analyze the constituent elements of the blockchain and start with the **blocks**. As we mentioned earlier, transactions are stored within the blockchain blocks, so each block is composed of two parts:

- A block **header**, in which the link to the previous block is stored in the form of a **hashing** checksum digest. This is done to prevent the possibility of altering the transactions stored in the previous block.
- A block **body**, containing the list of **transactions**, complete with relevant information (including the amount transferred, the addresses of peers, and so on).

The following diagram shows the structure of Bitcoin blocks and their mutual relationships within the blockchain:

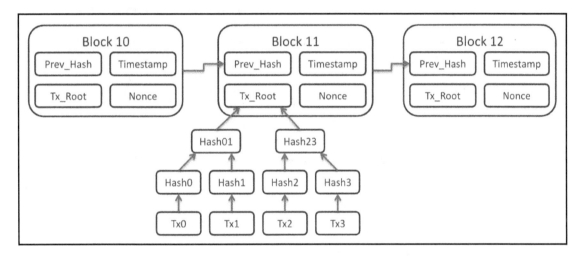

You can check out the image in the following link, `https://commons.m.wikimedia.org/wiki/File:Bitcoin_Block_Data.png`. As a consequence of how the blocks of the blockchain are structured, and by virtue of the reciprocal relationships that connect them, it is clear that both the transactions and the data that refer to them are immutable. This, however, does not mean that updates cannot be made to previous transactions; any changes will result in new transactions, which will, in turn, be validated and recorded within the blockchain in appending mode, thereby allowing the evolution of individual transactions to be reconstructed over time.

Unique addresses and transactions

We have already mentioned that, among the relevant information that's recorded within the blocks, there are the **addresses** of the counterparties of the transactions. These addresses are the unique identifiers that are needed to identify and distinguish between the counterparties involved in the transactions.

A **transaction** is, in fact, nothing but the transfer of an asset (monetary amount, right of use, or any other value) that is made between two addresses. To define these unique identifiers, cryptography is used – in particular, PKI – so the addresses are nothing but the public keys associated with the individual counterparts.

We often wonder if this addressing mechanism guarantees the anonymity of the counterparties of a transaction; in particular, we wonder whether the use of Bitcoins guarantees the anonymity of the users who use them.

To answer this question, it is necessary to distinguish between the functions that are performed by the addresses. This is done to uniquely identify the single counterpart of the transaction in terms of identifying the real physical subject that this unique identifier is associated with.

There is no doubt that the individual public keys are unique, but this does not exclude the possibility that the same user can generate a different public key for each individual transaction. Similarly, the end users are not directly identifiable from the public keys associated with them. To verify their real identity in a reliable way, they must be identified (verifying, for example, identity documents, and other biometric evidence), before allowing them to take part in transactions.

Nodes and consensus

Another important concept is that of a **node**.

Each node within the blockchain contributes to establishing or validating a transaction while making use of a predefined **consensus protocol** that's been specifically selected to guarantee the security and integrity of the blockchain (we will deal with the consensus mechanism in the final part of this chapter).

Now that we've introduced its building blocks, let's see how the blockchain actually works.

How Blockchain works

To realize the objectives that it was designed for, the blockchain must implement a series of mechanisms that involve not only computer science and cryptography, but also some concepts that come from other branches of scientific research (such as the use of theorems regarding game theory).

We have already mentioned that the main objective of the blockchain is to create a decentralized network, in which the individual nodes can carry out the functions that are traditionally in charge of a central authority. To achieve this result, we must ensure that the system is reliable in itself, without depending on the reliability of the single operators taking part in the network.

To this end, cryptography and game theory come together, united by the peer-to-peer network topology.

Guaranteeing traceability and block synchronization

Through the use of cryptography, it is possible to guarantee the traceability (non-repudiation) of a transaction to a specific counterparty. In the same way, it is possible to guarantee the integrity of the transaction by applying hashing algorithms.

The use of game theory performs another task. It ensures that all the nodes always have the updated synchronized copy of the ledger containing all the transactions.

One of the main problems that the Bitcoin blockchain has faced has been, for example, to prevent the possibility of double-spending; that is to say, that the same Bitcoin is not used simultaneously in two different transactions by the same counterparty.

To avoid this phenomenon, it is necessary that all the operators (nodes) are *on the same page*. This means that they all need to have the updated copy of the transaction database that all the operators must agree on. Therefore, the consensus on the history of transactions is achieved after the nodes agree on the status of the transaction database.

This requirement can be achieved by referring to a well-known theorem of game theory known as the Nash equilibrium (we will deal with consensus protocols later in this chapter).

Once the reliability and integrity of the transactions has been guaranteed, it is possible to share information within a decentralized and open network, thereby exploiting the typical characteristics of peer-to-peer networks.

The Blockchain process

Let's have a look at the process that characterizes the blockchain (in the description that follows, we will mostly refer to the Bitcoin blockchain).

The following diagram depicts the overall blockchain process:

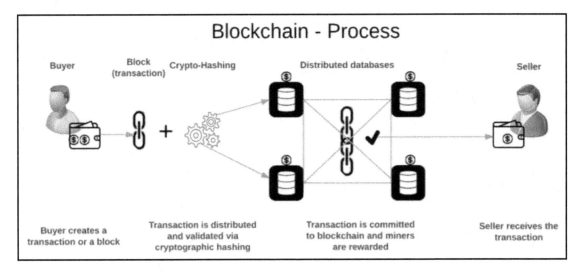

You can check out the image in the following link, `https://commons.m.wikimedia.org/wiki/File:Blockchain-Process.png`.

Let's take a look at the steps involved in this process:

1. The first step of the process consists of a node starting a transaction. This transaction is digitally signed with the private key associated with the same node that created the transaction.
2. At this point, the transaction is submitted for validation to other peers of the network (in Bitcoin, the peer nodes, called **miners,** are remunerated by assigning Bitcoins for this notarization task they perform).
3. Once validated, the transaction can be inserted into a block, which can be appended to the blockchain (the decision as to which block of which node must be inserted into the blockchain is determined by the consensus protocol).

4. Only after entering the block in the blockchain can the transaction be considered confirmed and become part of the shared ledger. The same block will receive a confirmation message from the subsequent block that will refer to it leveraging the **previous link** present in the block header. Transactions that haven't been confirmed yet are stored locally in a transaction pool, which, in the case of Bitcoins, is called **mempool**.

In this way, all the transactions that were undertaken beforehand are continuously reconfirmed by the new transactions that are inserted as successive blocks within the blockchain, thus realizing the immutability of the entire transaction chain.

Blockchain network topology

Now, let's look at the networking features of the blockchain.

The following diagram is a typical example of the centralized network topology, in which there is a central node that acts as a hub for sharing information with the other nodes:

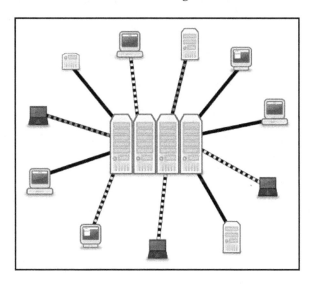

You can check out the image in the following link, `https://commons.m.wikimedia.org/wiki/File:NetworkCentral.svg`. The advantages of the centralized network can be summarized by the fact that there is only one central authority (server) that acts as an arbitrator. This manages the requests coming from the remaining nodes of the network (clients).

However, the fundamental limit of centralized networks is the fact that the central node represents a **single point of failure** for the entire network (which can, therefore, be the target of Denial of Service attacks, for example). If the central node is compromised, all information communication within the network is lost.

On the other hand, in a decentralized network, the control and management of information is distributed among the nodes that constitute the network, which act simultaneously both as the client and the server. This eliminates the single point of failure constituted by the central authority while improving efficiency in terms of information management.

Peer-to-peer networks are used to implement the decentralized blockchain network.

In a peer-to-peer network, there is no central node. Instead, each individual node can provide the remaining nodes with information that can be shared on the network:

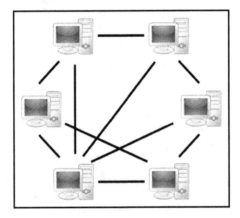

You can check out the image in the following link, `https://en.m.wikipedia.org/wiki/File:P2P-network.svg`. The decentralized model also allows each node to contribute to making relevant decisions regarding shared information (such as validating and inserting blocks representing transactions within the blockchain) through the implementation of the appropriate consensus protocols.

Network discovery and block synchronization

In the absence of a central node (authority) that acts as a hub in a peer-to-peer network, it is necessary to implement some indexation mechanism for the available resources, along with the network discovery methods, to allow the nodes to know who to contact to receive information.

Such resource indexing mechanisms are particularly important in the blockchain in order to allow for block synchronization.

In fact, we have seen that each node contains its own local copy of the blockchain – a copy that must be constantly synchronized with the global state present within the network.

To this end, every node that needs to be updated that resembles the global status of the blockchain sends information about the dimensions of its own local copy of the blockchain to others. Any node whose local copy of the blockchain is larger responds by sending information about the number of blocks to be added, thus allowing the node that needs to be updated to contact the peers it is connected to, in order to receive the missing blocks.

Now, let's look at the different types of blockchain.

Different types of blockchain

Following the recent developments in blockchain and the new research projects that have been proposed in recent years, we can distinguish between different types of blockchain.

In this section, we'll examine the most common types.

Public blockchains

First and foremost, we should tell public and private blockchains apart.

Public blockchains permit public access, therefore allowing anyone to participate in them since they are not the exclusive property of anyone. In technical terms, each participant in a public blockchain is authorized to receive a local copy of the shared ledger containing the transactions. Along with Bitcoin, which is the main (and most famous) public blockchain, Ethereum also falls into this category.

Private blockchains

Private blockchains, on the other hand, cannot be accessed by anyone. They are set up in order to share the transaction ledger within a small group of participants.

Permissioned blockchains

In the case of permissioned blockchains, access to the shared ledger is reserved exclusively for trusted counterparties.

A permissioned ledger is a blockchain where participants of the network are already known and trusted counterparties.

Despite the fact that verification of trusted counterparties is carried out by a central authority, in permissioned blockchains, it is still necessary to introduce a distributed consensus protocol. To validate the transactions, we need to introduce an alignment mechanism that keeps the local copies of the ledger synchronized with the global status of the transactions.

We must not confuse permissioned blockchains with private blockchains. A permissioned blockchain can also be public since it is sufficient to provide an access control mechanism that checks the credentials of the trusted counterparties before allowing access to the blockchain.

Distributed ledger technology

By definition, the blockchain consists of a shared distributed ledger; therefore, strictly speaking, all the various types of blockchain should fall under the definition of **distributed ledger technology** (**DLT**).

However, in order to distinguish the original blockchain (that is to say, the Bitcoin blockchain) from the other implementations that are inspired by it, we need to reserve the terminology of DLT to indicate specific technological solutions that are implemented in certain industrial sectors (such as the financial sector, logistics, and the supply chain that are designed to meet specific application and functional needs.

Similarly, the notion of DLT is becoming synonymous with permissioned blockchain, precisely because it represents specific solutions for specific sectors where access to the shared ledger is usually reserved for trusted counterparties.

Blockchain use cases

The presence of different types of blockchain is justified by the different goals (use cases) they are expected to achieve. Even the decision to implement a customized blockchain hides pitfalls that are often difficult to predict in the design phase, given the still experimental status of DLT technology.

Therefore, before adopting an experimental technology, it is necessary to be aware of whether it is actually necessary to use the blockchain to solve our project's functional and application tasks. It is also necessary to ask ourselves whether it is preferable to adopt existing solutions (such as Bitcoin, and Ethereum) instead of implementing a custom one. Among the challenges that we will face, the main one is to guarantee the adequate scalability of the technological solution.

Let's analyze some use cases in which the use of blockchain technology can be considered justified:

- **Financial Sector:** Undoubtedly, the sector that has been the most interested in the adoption of the blockchain technology is the financial sector (which includes payments, trading, financing, and so on).

  In particular, the spread of the blockchain coincided with the growing use of the **Initial Coin Offering** (**ICO**) by enterprises as a form of alternative financing, based on the use of cryptocurrencies instead of traditional equities.

  However, financial assets are not the only assets that can be transacted through the blockchain. Any asset or value, be it material or intangible (such as copyright, intellectual property, and know-how), can be an object of a transaction through blockchain in order to guarantee the protection of the rights of ownership to the legitimate owners.

- **Intellectual Property:** Since the very beginning of the internet and the web, copyright and intellectual property have been interested in the problem of protecting legitimate holders from possible violations due to online piracy.

  With the introduction of the blockchain, it is now possible to verify who has the legitimate right to exploit copyrights in order to prevent the possibility of abuse and piracy.

- **Internet of Things (IoT):** Other possible uses of the blockchain in the industrial sphere concern the emerging **Internet of Things** (**IoT**), in which the exchange of value assets is more easily managed by adopting a decentralized transaction and interchange model, rather than a traditional centralized model.
- **Supply Chains:** Similarly, the use of the blockchain is also growing in supply chains, for which the need to guarantee the necessary transparency in the production and distribution chain is of decisive importance.

- **Monetizing Personal Data:** Finally, citizens can also benefit from the introduction of the blockchain to monetize the use of their personal data, which is increasingly collected by the giants of the web (such as social media, for example). They can also solve problems regarding preservation of the confidentiality of their personal data, which is managed by both private companies and government agencies.

The use of the blockchain should allow more granular access to personal data, therefore limiting access to only indispensable information, thus preventing the indiscriminate use of personal data for unauthorized purposes.

From what we have said so far, it would be tempting to conclude that the adoption of blockchain technology brings only benefits; in reality, it is also important to understand the difficulties that characterize this technology, starting with the choice of the appropriate consensus protocol for establishing trust.

Establishing trust through consensus algorithms

As we mentioned in the previous paragraph, one of the main challenges we face in blockchain is to reach an agreement with all the counterparties regarding the validity of the transactions made, without having to resort to a central authority.

The blockchain adopts a collective coordination system, known as distributed consensus, which does not require centralized coordination.

This solution is inspired by the various examples that exist in nature regarding the collective coordination of independent individual behaviors, such as swarm intelligence, in order to reach a common goal (in the case of the blockchain, consent for the transactions being carried out).

On account of this, a collective decision-making process has to be introduced, in which all the nodes independently maintain a local copy of the transactions that are carried out, thus helping to determine the global status of the transaction history through a shared mechanism for reaching consensus.

Blockchain consensus layer

To reach a consensus on the global status of transactions, there is a dedicated application layer in the blockchain called the consensus layer. Obviously, the ways in which consent is achieved vary according to the different types of blockchain, so not all consensus mechanisms are suitable for all blockchains.

In the case of the Bitcoin blockchain, the mechanism for obtaining consent is based on the economic incentive. The nodes are encouraged to contribute to reaching consensus on transactions through their mining activity, with a view to receiving a reward in the form of Bitcoins. This incentive system is particularly important for public blockchains so that they can achieve and maintain the self-sustainability of the architecture itself.

Reaching consensus in the blockchain

Before analyzing the different consensus mechanisms available, we must distinguish between the different approaches that can be adopted for reaching consensus in the blockchain:

- Proof-based approach

- Consortium-based approach, also known as the permissioned approach

These approaches can be distinguished by the different ways in which consent is reached and by the type of blockchain to which they can be applied.

The proof-based approach is particularly useful for public and permissionless blockchains (such as Bitcoin and Ethereum), which are characterized by an indefinite number of nodes, while the consortium-based approach is used for permissioned blockchains, which are generally characterized by a reduced number of nodes.

In terms of scalability and speed in achieving consensus, there are differences between the two approaches. In the case of the proof-based approach, we have greater scalability with respect to the overall number of nodes, but at the expense of greater slowness, while in the case of the permissioned approach, the scalability is smaller, but consensus is reached more quickly. A typical example of a proof-based consensus mechanism, as we will see shortly, is **Proof of Work (PoW)**, which is used by both Bitcoin and Ethereum, which are the most notable examples of permissionless blockchains. Permissioned blockchains use other types of consensus mechanisms, such as **Proof of Authority (PoA)**.

Now, let's take a look at the characteristics of the PoW algorithm.

The basic logic of the PoW algorithm is to make adding a new block computationally expensive, thus reducing the possibility of being able to modify the transaction ledger.

In the presence of conflicting versions, the transaction whose amount of aggregated computational effort is greater than the others will be chosen as the transaction history. By applying the PoW criterion iteratively to all the nodes of the network, consensus will, therefore, be reached on the transaction history whose PoW is greater.

Now, let's look at the main consensus mechanisms that are available in more detail.

Understanding the consensus mechanisms

The purpose of the consensus mechanism is to allow the blockchain nodes to reach an agreement on the current state of transactions. The consensus mechanism must also be fault-tolerant, meaning that it must be able to function even in the presence of malfunctioning or dishonest nodes. This requirement leads us to the famous Byzantine Generals Problem, or Byzantine failure problem.

Byzantine Generals Problem

The Byzantine Generals Problem is a well-known dilemma about the difficulty of coordinating the decisions of several independent agents, whose most common formulation goes as follows. Imagine two generals of the Byzantine army who have to besiege the enemy fort located within a valley; the generals are on the two opposite hills of the valley and must coordinate their attack for it to succeed. In the event that the generals do not attack simultaneously, the attack will not succeed and their troops will be defeated by the enemy.

So, how can we synchronize the choice of the moment in which to attack at the same time, given that the communications between the generals must necessarily take place through the valley (or by traversing the enemy's field), with the possibility that some messengers can be captured, thus preventing their messages from reaching their destination?

The problem of the Byzantine generals arises in the blockchain in relation to the choice of a single version of the transaction history in the presence of nodes that cannot communicate correctly with others, or **dishonest** nodes that intend to cheat on the correct version of the transaction history, thus making the achievement of consensus within the network problematic. The consensus mechanism that is the most robust with respect to the problem of Byzantine generals is called **Byzantine fault tolerance** (**BFT**).

The PoW consensus mechanism also shows this capacity.

Proof of Work

In the PoW consensus mechanism, nodes must employ a high computational load to solve math challenges of increasing difficulty, in order to reach consensus on transactions. The problem of the Byzantine generals is solved by the fact that the PoW does not require the participation of all the nodes of the network. Also, there's no possibility of cheating since the math challenges that need to be solved are represented by hash codes that, by definition, cannot be reverse-engineered and therefore cannot be falsified (we will cover cryptographic aspects in more detail in Chapter 2, *Cryptography Essentials*).

The PoW, in fact, generates a hash code of a given length, and the goal of the nodes is to discover the input value that gave rise to this hash code. To solve this challenge, it is necessary to proceed by brute force (since the hash codes are not reversible); that is to say, it is necessary to proceed by trial and error. This determines a high computational load (work) on behalf of the single nodes. The node that finds the challenge's solution sends it to the rest of the network for verification by the other nodes (in the Bitcoin blockchain, these nodes receive Bitcoins as a reward for this activity).

As we mentioned in the previous paragraph, the logic of the PoW to make the addition of a new block computationally expensive, thus reducing the possibility of being able to modify the transaction ledger. Then, once the solution that's found by the node has been verified, the block it created can be inserted into the blockchain. The length of the blockchain increases accordingly, reflecting the computational effort (PoW) that was needed to reach this dimension. Therefore, the consensus that one of the blockchain local copies is the updated one is reached by selecting the longest chain, which is said to receive the **trust** of the network.

Given the characteristics of PoW, it is very difficult to modify a block (thus altering the underlying transaction) once it has been inserted into the blockchain, and the difficulty increases as the length of the chain increases. The advantages of PoW don't come free of cost, both in terms of time and the energy necessary to fulfill the required computational load.

To try to solve these disadvantages, the **Proof of Stake** (**PoS**) consensus mechanism was proposed.

Proof of Stake

In PoS, digital signatures are used instead of hash codes, and the node that's been authorized to create the next block to be included in the blockchain is selected on the basis of the amount of investment the node has made in the network.

At the same time, validator nodes are rewarded by receiving transaction fees for each validated block.

Proof of Authority

Unlike the previous mechanisms, **Proof of Authority (PoA)** is a consensus mechanism whose use is more appropriate in permissioned blockchains since it works with a limited number of transaction validator nodes. Consensus is reached on the basis of the greater trust attributed to these nodes.

Now that we've analyzed the main mechanisms that trust is established through in the blockchain, we will introduce the possible threats that put this trust at risk.

Potential threats that affect trust

The potential threats that might affect trust in the blockchain involve the following aspects:

- The blockchain distributed architecture
- The blockchain application layer
- The blockchain security model

Now, let's look at some of the main threats concerning these different aspects.

Threats to the distributed architecture

In general, the security threats concerning the blockchain are different compared to traditional applications, precisely because of the distributed nature of the blockchain architecture. Therefore, many of the attacks that are performed on centralized architectures are actually ineffective when performed on blockchain. Nonetheless, the latter suffers from vulnerabilities of its own.

One of the critical areas of the blockchain is the consensus mechanism, which presides over the integrity and reliability of transactions. Therefore, finding vulnerabilities that affect the consensus mechanism means undermining the trust of the blockchain.

These vulnerabilities, however, are more likely to be exploited in the blockchains with a restricted number of nodes, rather than in public blockchains (such as Bitcoin, which is more resistant to common attacks on the consensus mechanism).

51% attack

We have seen that the PoW consensus mechanism guarantees the achievement of consensus, even in the presence of non-functioning or dishonest nodes. However, if the dishonest node is able to control 51% of the computational capacity of the entire network, it is able to manipulate the transaction ledger at will (creating new blocks or modifying those that have already been inserted into the blockchain) without the need to obtain the consent of the network regarding the changes that have been made.

In this way, the dishonest node could prevent other nodes from adding blocks, thereby delaying the confirmation of transactions, or appropriating previously confirmed transactions.

Since the costs that are necessary to control 51% of the computational capacity of the network are likely to be much higher than the possible profit that can be made from doing this, a 51% attack can be performed to defeat the consensus mechanism, thereby affecting the blockchain's trust in order to achieve further goals.

Eclipse attacks

In addition to attacking the consensus mechanism, it is also possible to attack the distributed topology of the peer-to-peer network via the Eclipse attack. With this attack, it is possible to isolate single nodes from the rest of the network.

Due to this, the isolated node will not be able to receive reliable information from the rest of the network. Instead, it will receive information about the status of the network and transactions that have been distorted by the attacker.

Threats to the application layer

Instead of attacking the architecture of the blockchain, it is possible to exploit the vulnerabilities of the applications that are based on it, such as cryptocurrencies and smart contracts.

Cryptojacking

Through cryptojacking, the attacker tries to abuse the computational resources of a web or cloud-based service (or even of the user hosts) to transform them into mining pools, with the aim of reaching the computational capacity required by the PoW consensus mechanism for mining Bitcoins or other cryptocurrencies.

Attacking smart contracts

Smart contracts are self-enforced contracts that are developed in the form of software to be executed on the blockchain. One of the main platforms that smart contracts are developed on is Ethereum, which provides a specific virtual machine that these contracts are executed on.

Smart contracts on Ethereum are developed with the Solidity language; since this programming language is a complete Turing machine, it is subject to the presence of bugs in its applications, just like the other general-purpose programming languages. These programming bugs can be successfully exploited by an attacker who intends to steal or modify transactions that are managed through smart contracts.

Threats to the security model

The blockchain security model can also be subject to attacks.

To claim ownership over the assets that are managed through the blockchain, it is sufficient to show ownership of the private key associated with a given user (the public key being the unique address that's used to carry out the transactions). Therefore, if a user loses possession of their private key, they will no longer be able to prove they are the legitimate holder of the values that have been recorded in the transactions.

Similarly, after having successfully managed to steal a user's private key, an attacker will be able to impersonate the user (identity theft) within the blockchain. Therefore, it is extremely important to protect private keys by creating multiple backups on different devices.

Summary

In this chapter, we introduced the basic concepts of the blockchain and provided a reference framework regarding the topics we will cover in the following chapters. In particular, we have looked at the mechanisms that govern the achievement of consensus and trust within the blockchain and the possible threats in terms of security.

In the next chapter, we will introduce the cryptographic fundamentals that are used in the blockchain and fully understand their cyber security implications.

Cryptography Essentials 2

In this chapter, we will cover the fundamental notions of cryptography necessary to fully understand the security features of blockchain and **Distributed Ledger Technologies (DLTs)**. We'll outline the differences between symmetric and asymmetric cryptography, and we'll tell cryptography and hashing functions apart.

We will also explore some of the operations realized by the most prominent data structure implemented by blockchain, the Merkle tree, which exploits cryptography primitives to fulfill architectural core goals.

The topics we will cover in this chapter are the following:

- A glimpse into cryptography
- Symmetric versus asymmetric cryptography
- Elliptic cryptography in blockchain
- SHA hashing and digital signatures in practice
- Blockchain Merkle trees

Let's start our analysis with a glimpse into cryptography.

Technical requirements

The code files of this chapter can be found on GitHub:
https://github.com/PacktPublishing/-Securing-Blockchain-Networks-like-Ethereum-and-Hyperledger-Fabric/tree/master/Chapter02

Check out the following video to see the Code in Action: https://bit.ly/2UTN4PS

A glimpse into cryptography

Together with the decentralized network topography, the extensive use of cryptography is the other constitutive element that characterizes a blockchain. In particular, it is the adoption of asymmetric cryptography that allows a blockchain to achieve all of its advantages. In this chapter, we will briefly introduce symmetric cryptography, which will serve us to analyze asymmetric cryptography in depth, since it is the central aspect of a blockchain.

Let's now try to understand what aims cryptography must fulfill in general to then understand its role in the architecture of a blockchain.

The role played by cryptography

Historically, cryptography has been introduced to guarantee an adequate level of confidentiality for sensitive information.

There are examples of the use of cryptographic algorithms that date back to pre-Christian times (one of the most famous cryptographic algorithms is the algorithm of Caesar, which dates back to the eponymous Roman emperor, Julius Caesar).

If the guarantee of an adequate level of confidentiality is the main objective of cryptography, it is not its only objective. In recent times, the need to guarantee integrity, non-repudiation, and authenticity has emerged along with confidentiality.

Therefore, let's recapitulate the main goals that cryptography must fulfill:

- **Authenticity**: This consists of the possibility of reliably identifying the counterparties (sender and receiver) between which the exchange of sensitive information takes place.
- **Confidentiality**: This requirement results in the guarantee that the confidential information can be accessed exclusively by the authorized parties.
- **Integrity**: This consists of the possibility of verifying, if not preventing, the possibility of unauthorized changes to confidential information.
- **Non-repudiation**: This is the ability to unequivocally assess the authorship of a piece of content.

Usually, the confidentiality of sensitive information is achieved by applying the encryption algorithm to *plaintext*, which converts the plaintext into an encrypted format (ciphertext). For verifying the integrity of sensitive information, the algorithms used are also known as **trapdoor functions** and consist of hashing functions that calculate fingerprints (digest) associated with the information.

These functions are very reactive to changes, to the point that even a small change to the information determines a very different fingerprint being calculated by the hashing functions (hence making it clear that the information has been compromised). Authenticity and non-repudiation are usually achieved through signature mechanisms (digital signatures) exploiting the pairs of public and private keys generated with asymmetric cryptography algorithms.

After introducing the general purposes of cryptography, we will now look in more detail at the role played by cryptography within a blockchain.

Cryptography and the blockchain

The uses of cryptography (especially the functions offered by asymmetric cryptography) in the blockchain ecosystem are manifold.

In particular, through the use of public and private keys created using asymmetric cryptography, it is possible to uniquely identify the counterparties of a transaction within a blockchain (for example, the public keys are used in Bitcoins as unique addresses that identify their owner). Similarly, the private keys are used in digital signatures, allowing, in this way, to unequivocally establish the ownership of the assets exchanged in a transaction.

Equally important are the uses of hashing functions, adopted, for example, to determine the links between the blocks of the blockchain, making use of the `prev_hash` field within the block header (please refer to the *Blockchain building blocks* section in `Chapter 1`, *Introducing Blockchain Security and Attack Vectors*).

Furthermore, hashing functions are essential to guarantee the integrity of blockchain blocks, thereby preventing the possibility of any non-shared changes in the status of a transaction. Hashing functions are also used in consensus mechanisms such as the PoW, in particular, to address the Byzantine Generals' problem.

Cryptography is also used in the development of **Decentralized Applications (DApps)**.

Before analyzing symmetric and asymmetric cryptography in detail, we will now see some of the simplest encryption algorithms available.

Simple encryption example

Among the simplest examples of encryption algorithms, we can find the Caesar algorithm. Caesar's algorithm is an example of a substitution cipher, meaning that another character is substituted for a given character, respecting a certain coding rule in the substitution of the different characters.

In the following screenshot, we have reproduced one of the possible substitutions for letters of the alphabet. For our example, we'll choose the substitution that moves the original letter 12 positions to the right.

In this way, the letter A will correspond to the letter M, the letter B to the letter N, and so on:

Caesar algorithm substitution table of correspondence

Using the preceding encoding table, we can encrypt the plaintext by obtaining the corresponding ciphertext.

For example, the following message is in plaintext:

    HELLO WORLD

After the application of the substitution algorithm, the preceding would become the following ciphertext:

    TQXXA IADXP

The ciphertext hence obtained can then be sent to a trusted recipient, who will be able to decipher it (obtaining the original plaintext as output) using the same table of correspondence we used previously, but in the opposite direction.

The confidentiality of the plaintext is preserved by the fact that, even if the ciphertext should be intercepted by unauthorized subjects, they could not decipher the ciphertext without knowing the decoding table.

In the Caesar algorithm, the coding table can be replaced with the number of shifts occurring within the letters of the alphabet. This number of movements remains constant (in our case, it is 12 steps to the right of the letter A), and therefore constitutes the key used to encrypt the plaintext and obtain the ciphertext. To get back from the ciphertext to the original plaintext, we will not have to do anything but carry out the inverse procedure, that is to say, move to the left by 12 steps.

After having introduced the general concepts of cryptography, let's now look in more detail at the differences between symmetric and asymmetric cryptography.

Symmetric versus asymmetric cryptography

Symmetric cryptography is characterized by the fact that the same key is used both to encrypt plaintext (obtaining ciphertext as output) and to decipher the ciphertext (obtaining the original plaintext as output).

Asymmetric cryptography, on the other hand, is characterized by the introduction of two different keys, the public key and the private key, both associated by a mathematical relationship, which prevents or, at least, makes it very difficult in practice to trace back to the private key starting from the knowledge of the public key.

The two keys are therefore used to achieve different purposes: the public key is used to encrypt plaintext, while the corresponding private key is used to decipher the ciphertext.

Caesar's algorithm, which was introduced in the previous section, represents a very simple example of symmetric cryptography since the same encryption key is used both to encrypt and to decrypt. In the case of Caesar's algorithm, as we have seen, the key is the number of displacements required within the letters of the alphabet.

Symmetric encryption keys can take two different types:

- Stream ciphers
- Block ciphers

Let's look at the differences briefly.

Stream and block ciphers

The main difference between stream and block encryption algorithms is in the way the encryption of plaintext (and conversely, the decrypting of the ciphertext) is performed. With stream ciphers, the encryption is done one bit at a time. Ideally, to proceed with the encryption of the plaintext, it is possible to generate a sequence of pseudorandom bits to be used as an encryption key; in this way, each different bit corresponds to a different encryption key. Among the examples of stream ciphers are RC4, FISH, SNOW, and so on. In the case of block ciphers, on the other hand, the plaintext is divided into blocks of bits of fixed length (usually 64, 128, or 256 bits) to which the encryption key is applied. Examples of block ciphers include DES, 3DES, and AES.

In terms of efficiency, stream ciphers perform better than block ciphers, whereas block ciphers are appropriate for more general uses. In particular, since stream ciphers perform the encryption one bit at a time, they are more suitable for hardware-based encryption, while are not very well suitable for software-based encryption. Block ciphers, on the other hand, can be validly used both in software and hardware, even if they are not as efficient and fast as stream ciphers.

Although very efficient and robust, symmetric cryptography suffers from some important limitations from the point of view of key management, as we will see in the following subsection.

Symmetric cryptography limitations

The main weakness of symmetric cryptography is the management of encryption keys (also known as the **key distribution problem**). Since symmetric cryptography makes use of the same key to perform both the encryption and decryption processes, to establish reserved communication channels with multiple different counterparties we must, therefore, create and assign a different key to each individual counterpart. Consequently, the management of symmetric encryption keys does not scale well in distributed network contexts.

To realize this, it is sufficient to consider that in a network of n nodes, it would be necessary to create, distribute, and manage $n(n-1)/2$ different key pairs. Anyone who discovers the key used to encrypt the conversations established between two operators would, therefore, be able to decipher (and possibly even modify) the contents of these confidential conversations. Therefore, before establishing confidential communication, the trusted counterparties must share the encryption key securely, away from prying eyes (which is quite difficult to achieve using a non-reliable means of communication such as the internet).

Furthermore, the keys should be changed every time a new communication is established, to reduce the risk of reusing a previously used (and potentially compromised) key.

Asymmetric cryptography

To overcome these limitations, asymmetric cryptography was introduced.

The fundamental intuition behind asymmetric cryptography consists of separating the encryption process from the deciphering one, by using two different keys that are linked together by a mathematical relationship. As a consequence of this mathematical relationship, the knowledge of the key used to encrypt communications (the public key) is not sufficient to discover the key used to decipher communications (the private key). In this way, it is possible to publicly share the public key with an indistinct number of different operators, without having to create and assign a different encryption key to each individual counterpart (as in the case of symmetric encryption).

All of those interested in establishing a confidential channel of communication with a specific recipient will use the recipient's public key to encrypt communications, without worrying that the communications might be intercepted by third parties. Only the owner of the public key will be able to decrypt the communication's contents, using the private decryption key associated with the public key.

It should be noted that the introduction of asymmetric cryptography does not eliminate the need for symmetric cryptography; on the contrary, the two forms of cryptography complement each other. In fact, symmetric cryptography is more efficient in performing encryption, while asymmetric encryption allows better scalability of key management. For example, in an HTTPS/SSL communication, each client establishes a secure connection with the server using the server's SSL certificate. The SSL certificate contains the server's public key, with which each client will encrypt the information it will send back to the server. The private key (visible only to the server) associated with the public key is then used by the server to decrypt the data received from the clients. For efficiency reasons, once the secure connection has been established via the HTTPS protocol, a symmetric encryption key is then shared between the client and the server.

From this moment on, the exchange of information between the client and the server will then be encrypted with this symmetric key, hence exploiting the greater efficiency and speed typical of symmetric encryption with respect to asymmetric encryption.

Asymmetric key management with PKI

The key distribution problem for asymmetric encryption is therefore reduced to assuring the safety of only the private key. However, there remains a problem to be solved: how can we ensure that the public key we are using to guarantee the confidentiality of communications actually belongs to the recipient of our messages and not to an intruder, who could intercept our communication? To this end, a trusted third party is normally introduced who assumes the role of authority in ensuring the authenticity of the public key and its ownership to an identified subject.

A **Public Key Infrastructure** (**PKI**) is therefore established, which takes care of issuing security certificates, signed by the Certification Authority, which guarantees the validity and traceability of public keys to the entities to which these certificates belong. We will see in the *SHA hashing and digital signatures in practice* section of this chapter how the PKI process translates into the blockchain, which by definition tends to eliminate all central authorities, assigning notarization functions to the distributed network as a whole.

Now, instead, we will examine more closely how public and private key pairs are generated and their practical use in message encryption and decryption. To this end, we will show the first and most widespread of the asymmetric cryptography algorithms, the RSA algorithm.

Understanding RSA from scratch

The RSA algorithm owes its name to the three cryptanalysts who invented it, namely, Ron Rivest, Adi Shamir, and Leonard Adleman. RSA is the most widespread asymmetric encryption algorithm in the world, and its security is based on the fact that, mathematically, it is practically very difficult (if not impossible) to perform the factorization (the reduction of an integer number into its prime factors) of very large numbers without requiring thousands of years of computation time.

In other words, while it is very simple to multiply together two prime numbers of arbitrary size, the inverse operation of reducing the resulting product to its prime factors (factorization) requires a very long time, considering the current computational capacities.

The RSA algorithm can be considered a block cipher since the input is usually divided into blocks and the encryption keys typically take on a size between 1,024 and 4,096 bits. The encryption times grow as the size of the encryption keys increases.

To fully understand how the RSA algorithm works, we must first briefly mention the mathematical operations of modular arithmetic and the extended Euclidean algorithm.

Modular arithmetic

Intuitively, modular arithmetic operations can be described by referring to a clock: the hours of the day are, in fact, measured by performing modular arithmetic operations in module 12, which means that the clock restarts counting the hours from 1 each time that it exceeds 12 hours. At the end of the day, the clock will have completed two full turns, and 24 hours is represented by two complete turns of 12 hours each.

In other words, 13.00 hours corresponds to the value 1 on the clock.

Formally, it is possible to represent this value using the following formula:

```
13 (mod 12) = 1
```

In practice, the module operation returns the remainder of the division between the number 13 and the argument of module 12. Using the Python scripting language, the module operation can be shown by executing the following statement:

```
>>> 13 % 12
>>> 1
```

Here, the Python operator, %, represents the modulus operation.

In general, given an integer, A, the number B can be considered an inverse of the number A in the form M, if it is possible to issue the following mathematical relationship:

```
A x B = 1 (mod M)
```

The previous relationship can also be expressed as follows:

```
A x B - 1 = C x M
```

Here, C is a multiplicative factor of the modulus, M.

Showing a concrete numerical example, we can say that the number 5 (B) is the inverse of the number 3 (A) in modulus 7 (M) since it is possible to establish the following relations:

```
3 x 5 = 1 (mod 7)
```

```
3 x 5 - 1 = 2 x 7
```

Here, the multiplicative factor, C, in this case, assumes the value of 2.

Anyway, to determine whether a number has inverse modulus values, we have to resort to the extended Euclidean algorithm.

The extended Euclidean algorithm

The extended Euclidean algorithm is a variant of the Euclidean algorithm. With the Euclidean algorithm, we can determine when A has an inverse module M, verifying the following equation:

```
gcd(A, M) = 1
```

Here, **gcd** stands for the **Greatest Common Divisors** operation. However, this equation does not allow us to determine whether an arbitrary number has inverse modulus values. We must, therefore, resort to the extended Euclidean algorithm.

For a Python implementation of the extended Euclidean algorithm, please refer to this link: `https://en.wikibooks.org/wiki/Algorithm_Implementation/Mathematics/Extended_Euclidean_algorithm` (the code is released under the Creative Commons License: `https://creativecommons.org/licenses/by-sa/3.0/`).

We will see the extended Euclidean algorithm in action in the next subsection. Having clarified the preliminary mathematical concepts, we are now able to understand how the RSA algorithm works.

RSA algorithm implementation

As we have seen, asymmetric encryption algorithms are characterized by the use of two different keys: the public key, which is used to encrypt (convert plaintext into ciphertext), and the private key, which is used to decrypt (convert ciphertext into the original plaintext). Therefore, the first task to complete is to create the public and private key pair in a way that guarantees that it is not feasible to trace the corresponding private key (which must remain secret) from the knowledge of the public key (which is freely available to anyone).

To create the keys pair, we will, therefore, use the mathematical features associated with the factorization in prime numbers of integer numbers and modular arithmetic operations.

As we know, current computational capabilities are not fit for the factorization of large numbers in a reasonable amount of time (the discourse changes when the quantum computer is available, as we will see in the `Chapter 3`, *Blockchain Security Assumptions*).

We can then select a sufficiently large number by multiplying two prime numbers chosen at random and assume this product as the maximum value. This maximum value will be used to define our public and private keys, which will be represented by two numeric values falling in the range between 0 and the maximum value. The maximum value also represents the modulus argument for the encrypting process, which is implemented by multiplying the plaintext by several times equal to the value of the public key. If the result of this operation exceeds the maximum value, we will have to calculate the module using the maximum value as an argument.

Let's see what all of this means in practical terms.

Generating RSA keys

To generate the keys, we then choose two prime numbers, P and Q, and calculate their product, N:

```
N = P x Q
```

In numerical terms, supposing that P = 7 and Q = 13, we will obtain the product:

```
N = 7 x 13 = 91
```

The N value (equal to 91) therefore represents our maximum value.

Now, let's choose an encryption exponent, E, that respects the following condition:

```
gcd (E, (P - 1) x (Q - 1)) = 1
```

We choose E = 5, therefore, the previous condition becomes as follows:

```
gcd (5, (7 - 1) x (13 - 1)) = 1

gcd (5, 6 x 12) = 1
```

We can verify this condition by running a simple Python script at Command Prompt:

```
>>> import math
>>> print math.gcd (5, 72)
>>> 1
```

At this point, once the previous condition has been successfully verified, we can assume E (our encryption exponent) as our public key; therefore, we have the following:

```
public_key = E = 5
```

We now need to calculate the private key associated with this public key. This is where the extended Euclidean algorithm comes into play.

In fact, to get our private key, D, we will have to meet the following condition:

```
E x D = 1 (mod (P - 1) x (Q - 1))
```

This can be rewritten as follows:

```
E x D = 1 (mod (7-1) x (13-1))
```

In other terms, we have the following:

```
E x D = 1 (mod 72)
```

Therefore, the value of D we need is just the inverse modulus of E in modulus 72.

To obtain the value of D, we therefore use the extended Euclidean algorithm, leveraging the Python implementation that we indicated in the previous subsection, *The extended Euclidean algorithm*:

```
import XCGD

p = 7
q = 13
e = 5
m = (p-1)*(q-1)
d = XCGD.xgcd(e,m)[1]

print ("Inverse Modulus of " + str(e) + " in modulus " + str(m) + " = " +
str(d) )

Inverse Modulus of 5 in modulus 72 = 29
```

The value of D calculated with the extended Euclidean algorithm is therefore 29; this value corresponds to the private key associated with the public key, E:

```
private_key = D = 29
```

Now, let's see how to proceed with the encryption and decrypting using the pair of keys just created.

Encrypting and decrypting with RSA keys

To encrypt a message using the public key, we must first convert the message into its numerical format (for example, using the UTF-8 encoding, as we will see in a moment).

It is necessary to verify that the message in numerical format is not greater than the module N associated with the public key (by verifying that it does not exceed the maximum value, represented by the product $P \times Q$ - in our example, 91).

To calculate the ciphertext, we must then raise the plaintext to the power of the exponent E (the public key) in modulus N, with the following formula:

$cipher = plain^E (mod\ N)$

The reverse decrypting operation consists of raising the ciphertext to the power of the exponent D (the private key, in module N):

$plain = cipher^D (mod\ N)$

Let's assume we want to encrypt the HELLO plaintext with the public key.

The first thing we need to do is convert the plaintext into a numeric format using the UTF-8 code, as shown in the following table:

A	B	C	D	E	F	G	H	I	J	K	L	M	N	O	P	Q	R	S	T	U	V	W	X	Y	Z
65	66	67	68	69	70	71	72	73	74	75	76	77	78	79	80	81	82	83	84	85	86	87	88	89	90

UTF-8 encoding

Encoding the HELLO string with UTF-8 would return the following:

H	E	L	L	O
72	69	76	76	79

HELLO in UTF-8 encoding

We then encrypt every single numerical value of the plaintext by applying the public key, using the following formula:

$plain^E (mod\ N)$

To apply the formula to every numerical value, we can use a simple Python script:

```
cipher = []
cipher.append(72**5 % 91)
```

```
cipher.append(69**5 % 91)
cipher.append(76**5 % 91)
cipher.append(76**5 % 91)
cipher.append(79**5 % 91)

print("Ciphertext: ", cipher)
```

This produces the following `Ciphertext` values:

```
Ciphertext:  [11, 62, 20, 20, 53]
```

To decipher the ciphertext and get the original plaintext, we need to apply the private key to the ciphertext, using the following formula:

$plain = cipher^D (mod\ N)$

Again, we can resort to a simple Python script:

```
plain = []
plain.append(cipher[0]**29 % 91)
plain.append(cipher[1]**29 % 91)
plain.append(cipher[2]**29 % 91)
plain.append(cipher[3]**29 % 91)
plain.append(cipher[4]**29 % 91)

print("Plaintext:  ", plain)
```

Hence, we obtain the original plaintext:

```
Plaintext:  [72, 69, 76, 76, 79]
```

As a closing remark, remember that the security of the RSA algorithm depends on the difficulty of obtaining the private key D from the public key E, due to the computational infeasibility of factorizing large numerical values into prime numbers. However, it is possible to use other mathematical features for the creation of asymmetric cryptographic keys, such as the discrete logarithm problems in finite fields, of which elliptic cryptography represents a generalized version, as we will see in the next section.

Elliptic cryptography in blockchain

Elliptic-Curve Cryptography (ECC) represents an alternative way of implementing asymmetric cryptography. ECC is based on the discrete logarithm problem since it is considered to be more secure for generating cryptographic keys when it is applied to elliptic curves.

The discrete logarithm problem

In particular, the safety of ECC is based, on one hand, on the simplicity of calculating a multiplication starting from a given point (known as the point generator) on an elliptic curve, and on the other hand, on the infeasibility of obtaining the multiplicand given the point generator and the product result.

In other words, given two points, P and Q, the discrete logarithm problem is reduced to finding the integer N that satisfies the equation $Q = N \times P$. This difficulty is related to the problem of finding the discrete logarithm of a random elliptic curve with respect to a fixed base point, and the difficulty of the problem is determined by the size of the elliptic curve.

Besides the greater security associated with the difficulty of solving the discrete logarithm problem, the keys generated with ECC show another advantage, constituted by their greater computational efficiency.

RSA versus ECC keys

Compared to traditional algorithms such as RSA, ECC makes it possible to create smaller keys, with obvious advantages both in terms of computational efficiency and the required working memory.

In the following screenshot, we see a comparison between the different sizes of the RSA and ECC keys to achieve the same level of security:

RSA size (in bits)	ECC size
1024	160
2048	224
3072	256
7680	384
15360	521

RSA versus ECC keys

However, ECC is mainly used in the management of key exchange and digital signatures, rather than in encryption. Even in the case of ECC, once a secure key exchange protocol has been established between two counterparts, it is possible to share a symmetric encryption key to carry out efficient communication encoding.

Elliptic curves math properties

From a mathematical point of view, an elliptic curve is represented by the following equation, which describes a plane curve over a finite field (a field with a finite number of elements defined by an arbitrary prime number):

$$y^2 = x^3 + ax + b$$

When domain parameters a and b vary, the elliptic curve takes different forms, as in the following diagram, in which the parameters take the values $a = -1$ and $b = 1$.

The following shows an elliptic curve with $a = -1$ and $b = 1$:

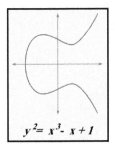

You can check out the image at, `https://commons.wikimedia.org/wiki/File:ECClines-3-2.svg`. Also, here is the license for the image: `https://creativecommons.org/licenses/by-sa/3.0/deed.en`.

From the analysis of the graph of the elliptic curve, we can immediately notice some important characteristics:

- First, an elliptic curve is characterized by the absence of singularity, meaning that there are neither cusps nor self-intersections in the curve graph.
- Furthermore, the elliptic curves are symmetric with respect to the x-axis (since the curve equation implies the calculation of the y square).
- Last but not least, the most interesting property of the elliptic curve is that if a nonvertical line intersects two points in the curve, it will always intersect a third point as well.

This last property is quite important, as it is used in ECC to create public keys from a private key.

To understand the mechanism of the derivation of public keys as points lying on the elliptic curve, we must first introduce some concepts related to abelian groups.

Abelian groups

In general, a group, G, consists of a set of elements on which an operation is defined for which the following four properties are respected:

- It is closed.
- It is associative.
- There is an identity element.
- There is an inverse for every element.

If the group also respects the commutative property, it is said to be an **abelian group**.

To better understand the properties of abelian groups, let's take as an example the arithmetic operation of addition, conventionally denoted by the symbol +, and verify the previous properties for a hypothetical group, G:

- **Closure**: If P and Q are elements of G, then the result of the addition, $P + Q$ (their sum), also belongs to G.
- **Associativity**: $(P + Q) + R = P + (Q + R)$
- There must be an identity element 0 so that $P + 0 = 0 + P = P$
- There must be an inverse for every element so that $P + Q = 0$.
- **Commutativity**: $P + Q = Q + P$

It is easy to verify that the set of integers is an abelian group, as all of the preceding five properties are met with respect to the operation of addition.

Virtually all of the groups used in cryptography are abelian groups, as it is precisely the respect of the commutative property that makes them useful for performing cryptographic operations. Furthermore, once the first four fundamental properties of the groups have been verified, other properties derive from them as a logical consequence (such as the uniqueness of the identity element and the inverses).

Abelian groups for elliptic curves

Now, let's see how to verify the properties of the abelian groups for elliptic curves, with respect to the addition operation on a hypothetical set, G:

- **Closure**: The points of an elliptic curve are the elements of the set G.
- **Identity element**: As the identity element, we introduce a point at infinity as part of the elliptic curve and denote it with the symbol 0.
- **An inverse for every element**: Due to the symmetry property of elliptic curves, every point has its inverse with respect to the x-axis.

We still need to verify the associative and commutative properties; before proceeding to their verification, we must define the addition operation for three aligned points on the elliptic curves. The operation of adding three points P, Q, and R (all of them different from zero), aligned on the elliptic curve, is as follows:

$$P + Q + R = 0;$$

This condition means that the sum of three points aligned on the elliptic curve is zero.

From this condition, it follows the irrelevance of the order of the addends, so it is possible to rewrite the operation of adding the three aligned points in the following equivalent forms:

$$P + (Q + R) = 0;$$
$$Q + (P + R) = 0;$$
$$R + (P + Q) = 0;$$

In this way, we have verified the respect of both the associative and commutative properties.

In the following screenshot, we can see some examples of point additions on the elliptic curve:

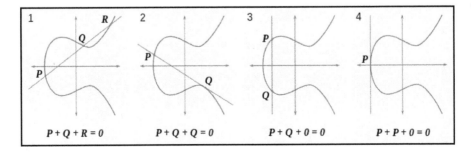

You can check out the image at, `https://commons.wikimedia.org/wiki/File:ECClines.svg`.

Let's now see how to leverage ECC to generate public keys.

Generating public keys with ECC

Among the various operations definable on elliptic curves, the one of particular interest for cryptography is the multiplication operation. As in the case of addition, multiplication on elliptic curves also takes on a special definition. To realize this, let's consider a simple example of multiplication, also known as point doubling, described graphically in the following diagram.

The following shows point doubling on an elliptic curve:

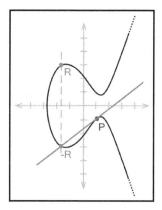

You can check out the image at, `https://commons.wikimedia.org/wiki/File:Doubling_P.PNG`. Also, here is the license for the image: `https://en.wikipedia.org/wiki/en:public_domain`.

To perform the point doubling operation, we need to accomplish the following steps:

- Trace the tangent to the elliptic curve in the point, *P* (the point generator).
- The tangent will intersect the elliptic curve at the point -*R*.
- By virtue of the symmetry of the curve with respect to the *x*-axis, we reverse the point, -*R*, in its inverse, *R*.
- The *R* point hence represents the multiple of 2 of the point generator, *P*, in other words, *R* = 2*P*, as a result of the point doubling operation.

Now, let's see how to use the point doubling operation to generate the public key starting from the private key.

To find a point on the elliptic curve that is a multiple, *N*, of the point generator, *P*, we can repeat the operation of point doubling *N* times. Similarly, to calculate the public key associated with the private key, we repeat the point doubling operation starting from a predefined point generator, *P*, several times equal to the numeric value represented by the private key. In practice, to get the public key we must multiply *P* by our private key, bouncing around the elliptic curve a private key number of times. The Cartesian coordinates of the point hence identified on the elliptic curve will, therefore, correspond to our public key.

It should be noted that the operation of point doubling performed on an elliptic curve represents a **trapdoor** (not invertible) function - a function that is simple to calculate in one sense, but difficult to invert.

Other examples of non-invertible trapdoor functions are hash functions, which we will cover in the following section.

SHA hashing and digital signatures in practice

A hash function is an encryption algorithm that allows you to map a set of data of arbitrary size into a corresponding numerical value of predetermined size, also called a **hash value** (or **digest**). The particularity of hash functions is that they are not invertible (also known as one-way or trapdoor functions).

Unlike the encrypting process, in which it is always possible to pass from the ciphertext to the original plaintext by applying the decryption key, in the case of hash functions, it is not possible to obtain the original dataset starting from the hash value, even knowing the algorithm that has generated it. By virtue of this property, hash functions are commonly used to verify data integrity, as hash values are very sensitive to changes in input data.

Even a small change in the input data causes the generation of a completely different hash value (with respect to the one calculated on the original input data), hence permitting to immediately detect the presence of a change in the input data.

Now, let's look at the characteristics of cryptographic hash functions.

Cryptographic hash function characteristics

Cryptographic hash functions constitute a subset of hash functions, used specifically to fulfill the purposes of cryptography. As hash functions, cryptographic hash functions, too, are non-invertible functions (one-way functions) that allow associating to a set of input data of arbitrary length a numeric value of predetermined length called a hash value or message digest.

Nonetheless, the main properties that cryptographic hash functions must respect are the following:

- It must be possible to associate a hash value to any input string of arbitrary length.
- It must be possible to efficiently calculate the hash value for any input given.
- The output produced by the algorithm must be deterministic, meaning that when feeding the algorithm with the same input data, the returned hash value must remain the same.
- The algorithm is not invertible, so it is not possible to obtain the input data starting from the hash value output.
- The algorithm must be sensitive to even the smallest changes, consequently generating a hash value that cannot be correlated to the changes made.
- The algorithm must be collision-resistant, so it is very unlikely that two different sets of data input will give rise to the same hash value.

After presenting the features of the hash functions, let's see their use in blockchain.

Hash functions in blockchain

The use of hash functions in blockchain is widespread, as they are involved in the implementation of many of blockchain's core mechanisms. Precisely because of their non-invertibility, hash functions are used to create a unique identifier to be associated with each block, calculating its hash value and saving it in the `Prev_Hash` field of the block header. In this way, each block is linked to the previous one through a reference to the hash value calculated on the previous block.

The integrity of the chain of blocks (blockchain) that is hence created is guaranteed by the fact that it is not possible to modify a block without altering its hash value, and since hash values are very sensitive even to the slightest changes, any changes on the block would give rise to a completely different hash value.

The other uses of hash functions in the blockchain concern the implementation of the PoW consensus algorithm and the generation of addresses and digital signatures, as we shall see in the following sections.

Before addressing these topics, let's look at some of the most common hashing algorithms.

Hashing algorithms

Among the most commonly used hashing algorithms, we find the algorithms of the Message Digest (MD) and Secure Hash Algorithms (SHA) families.

The algorithms of the MD family represent the oldest hashing algorithms; they are still used for practical reasons (given the simplicity of their use) even if they are no longer considered sufficiently secure for current needs. The most common algorithm of the MD family is the MD5, which produces a 128-bit message digest (represented by an output string of 32 hexadecimal digits), by consuming input data in 512-bit blocks.

The algorithms of the MD family have over time been substituted by the algorithms of the SHA family, represented by the four algorithms SHA-0, SHA-1, SHA-2, and SHA-3, since they are considered safer than MD.

We will deal with SHA algorithms in the next section.

SHA algorithms

Originally, the first algorithm of the family was simply known as SHA; following the discovery of some security problems, the SHA-1 version was introduced and the original version was discontinued and renamed SHA-0. Even for the SHA-1 version, however, a vulnerability was discovered in 2005 that allowed the identification of collisions in digests. To overcome these vulnerabilities, the SHA-2 version was introduced, which is actually a separate family of hash functions, as they allow the creation of digests of different sizes.

The main difference between SHA-256 and SHA-512 is that the first algorithm is implemented using 32-bit words, while the second one exploits 64-bit words.

The SHA-256 version is widespread and is currently used in Bitcoin's blockchain as a hashing algorithm in the implementation of the PoW consensus protocol.

The latest and most recent version is SHA-3, which is not a replacement for the SHA-2 version, but complements it.

In terms of efficiency, the performance of SHA-2 proves better in software implementations, while SHA-3 performs better than SHA-2 when it comes to hardware-embedded implementation.

Now, let's see the different hashing algorithms in action.

Hashing examples

We can see the different hashing algorithms in action using the utilities available as executable applications for different operating systems (Windows, Linux, and macOS) or using a scripting language such as Python, which provides us with a specific function library, hashlib, for the calculation and verification of hash digests.

In the example code that follows, we will show how to use the Python hashlib library to compare the md5 and sha256 hashing algorithms, showing how even minimal changes (such as simply changing the first letters of the words from uppercase to lowercase) in the input data give rise to completely different digests for both algorithms:

```
-*- coding: utf-8 -*-
import hashlib

md  = hashlib.md5()
sha = hashlib.sha256()

# md5 Uppercase first letters
md.update("Hello World".encode('utf-8'))
print (md.hexdigest())

# md5 Lowercase first letters
md.update("hello world".encode('utf-8'))
print (md.hexdigest())

# sha Uppercase first letters
sha.update("Hello World".encode('utf-8'))
print (sha.hexdigest())

# sha Lowercase first letters
sha.update("hello world".encode('utf-8'))
print (sha.hexdigest())
```

Here, we show the script output:

```
b10a8db164e0754105b7a99be72e3fe5
1901c730c33947ecc7f26716dfd84cff
a591a6d40bf420404a011733cfb7b190d62c65bf0bcda32b57b277d9ad9f146e
411e8b283045feeb2f3dcc4492fee2e2f29c8c7a620eb7c8069ffcfcde3115b3
```

We can see from the script output that even the slightest modification in the input string leads to a completely different result in the digests produced by both the md5 and sha256 algorithms.

Digital signatures and DSA

In the previous sections, we saw the advantages of asymmetric cryptography compared to symmetric cryptography, as far as key management is concerned. However, even though asymmetric cryptography can be used for encryption, it does not permit us to obtain the same performance as symmetric cryptography does. The greater utility of asymmetric cryptography hence consists of achieving further cryptographic goals, such as the creation of digital signatures.

A digital signature is a proof of ownership that can be applied to digital content. Taking advantage of the mathematical relationship between the public key and the corresponding private key, the owner of digital content may sign it with a private key and, once signed, send it to the intended recipient. The recipient of the digitally signed content may verify the ownership of the content by applying the sender's public key (which is publicly available to anyone) to the signed content.

Since nobody can create the digital signature without holding the private key (which is secretly kept by its legitimate owner, the digital signature is, therefore, a valid proof of ownership.

The **Digital Signature Algorithm (DSA)**, originally designed by the NSA, and based on discrete logarithms, was introduced to achieve the following:

- Digitally signed content authenticity, via private key signing and public key verification

- Data integrity, via hashing computation and digest verification
- Non-repudiation, achieved via both authenticity and data integrity, preventing disputes over digitally-signed transactions

We have hereby completed the picture of the features offered by asymmetric cryptography; now, we will see how these features are used to store and manage transaction data, introducing the main data structure implemented in the blockchain, the Merkle tree.

Blockchain Merkle trees

A **Merkle tree** is a binary tree data structure (meaning that each parent has at most two children nodes), where the leaf nodes contain the hash digests of the data blocks, and parent nodes contain the hash digest calculated on the hashes of its children. The process of hashing terminates when the root of the tree is reached.

Data integrity is guaranteed by the root hash value: if one of the nodes were to be modified, the digest associated with the root would change radically, by virtue of the sensitivity of the hash functions to even the slightest changes in input data.

The Merkle tree is particularly useful in the blockchain as it allows us to store sets of data by calculating a hash digest for each dataset, hence synthesizing all of the transactions contained in each block. The implementation of Bitcoin's Merkle tree uses SHA-256 as a hash function, which we introduced in the section *SHA algorithms*.

Now, let's see how to keep a binary Merkle tree balanced.

The following diagram shows a fully balanced Merkle tree:

You can check out the image at, `https://raw.githubusercontent.com/vpaliy/merklelib/master/ext/merkle.jpg`.

The following diagram shows an *artificially* balanced Merkle tree, in which an empty light-weight node (dummy node) was added to keep it balanced since the tree shows a number of leaves that are not a power of two:

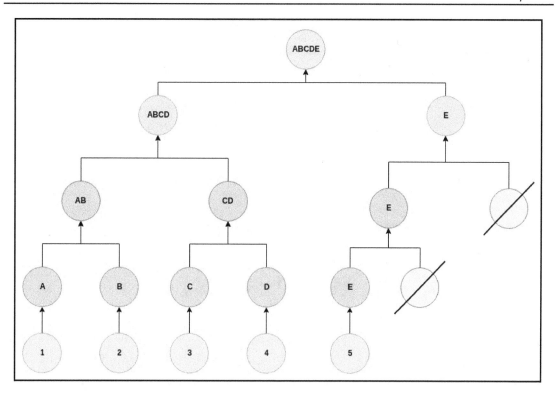

You can check out the image at, `https://raw.githubusercontent.com/vpaliy/merklelib/` `master/ext/empty.jpg`.

The moment we need to add a new node to the tree, we simply replace the dummy node with the real one and then recalculate the hash value associated with the root.

A Merkle tree audit proof

One of the most frequent operations that takes place on a Merkle tree is to verify the presence of a specific element within the tree, by issuing an audit proof on the Merkle tree.

The following diagram shows how a Merkle tree audit proof works:

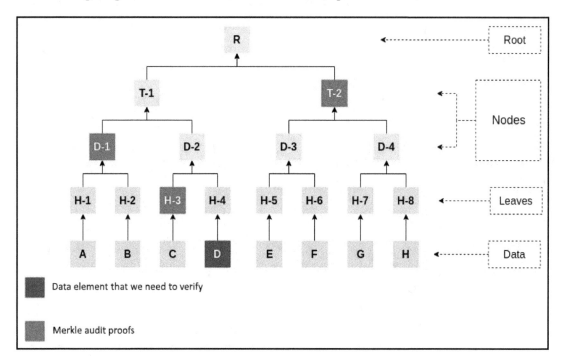

You can check out the image at, https://raw.githubusercontent.com/vpaliy/merklelib/master/ext/proof.jpg.

Suppose we want to check the presence of element **D** inside the Merkle tree. Since we already have the hash value associated with **D** (alternatively, we can simply calculate it), we need to trace the tree back through the sibling node and reach the root.

In other words, we need to identify the **H-3** element to calculate the hash value associated with the **D-2** element, and once the **D-2** element is calculated, we need to identify the **D-1** element to calculate the hash value associated with the **T-1** element and so on, up to the root.

Merkle tree consistency proof

Another operation that can be performed on a Merkle tree is consistency proof, aimed at verifying whether two different versions of the archive are consistent with each other, checking whether the next version of the database includes all of the data (the transactions) contained in the previous version.

The elements must also respect the temporal order of insertion. It appears evident at this point how the audit proof and the consistency proof both resemble operations required to achieve the global consensus on a blockchain status.

To understand the tasks accomplished by a Merkle tree and the operations that can be performed on it, let's now analyze an example of a Merkle tree implementation in Python.

Implementing a Merkle tree

We'll now look at a practical example of a Merkle tree implementation, using the Python library, merklelib, released under MIT license (https://opensource.org/licenses/MIT) and available for download on GitHub at https://github.com/vpaliy/merklelib/.

To install the merklelib library, we can proceed with the following command:

```
pip install merklelib
```

Alternatively, we can clone the source code available on GitHub using the git utility and proceed with the manual installation:

```
$ git clone git clone https://github.com/vpaliy/merklelib.git
```

The following Python example code creates and populates a Merkle tree, then verifies leaf inclusion, performs an audit proof for a specific element, and does a consistency check by comparing two different trees.

Let's see these operations in sequence, starting with verifying the inclusion in the tree of the leaves corresponding to the elements, C and E, by generating an audit proof for each of them:

```
import string
import hashlib

from merklelib import MerkleTree, beautify

data = ('A','B','C','D')

# build a Merkle tree for the data
tree = MerkleTree(data)

# generate an audit proof for the element 'C'
proof = tree.get_proof('C')

# now verify that C is in the tree
if tree.verify_leaf_inclusion('C', proof):
```

```
  print('C is in the tree')
else:
  print('C is not in the tree')

# generate an audit proof for the element 'E'
proof = tree.get_proof('E')

# now verify that E is not in the tree
if tree.verify_leaf_inclusion('E', proof):
  print('E is in the tree')
else:
  print('E is not in the tree')
```

Let's now perform a consistency check, by checking whether the newly created tree contains the same items and in the same order as the old one:

```
new_data = ('E','F','G','H')
new_tree = MerkleTree(new_data)

if tree == new_tree:
  print('Versions are consistent')
else:
  print('Versions are different')
```

The code example terminates by displaying the tree data structure in the terminal:

```
# display the tree in the terminal
print("display the tree:\n")
beautify(tree)
```

This is the output for the complete script:

```
C is in the tree
E is not in the tree
Versions are different
display the tree:

5c8dc617d287a4297eb2bcb81b37644b5138e57ad461c657db152109e3fc9fca
├── ed692f01f7f6c46930d7ad8f9adad3f9f38b7379cf6a8d2f399a0ba1e914fe25
│   ├── c00b4d3c929cb5cc316691ed4636f634576f2c9b2954767234c5274e9dde185d
│   └── 87afe6086fe4571e37657e76281301f189c75ebae1d2eaafb56d578067a1d95e
└── d62c77efa9be96355bb8b07aefc985914377de5aec1287998c9a10f11cd8d075
├── b563a5e69628743929eddec0ccfeb0745c39577e12a72e84915edd6633cb97f2
└── 08a2afecc9feaef6737f055c177a56a363d28a78d7b259b8c5f66b32174f2e7d
```

With Merkle trees, we have completed our journey in cryptography essentials.

Summary

In this chapter, we have addressed the cryptographic aspects necessary to understand the core mechanisms of blockchain and DLTs. We focused in particular on asymmetric cryptography, used extensively in the implementation of the functionalities of the blockchain, analyzing in detail the implementation of the RSA algorithm, which constitutes the reference model of the PKI architecture.

We then looked at an alternative solution in the generation and validation of asymmetric keys, consisting of the use of elliptic curve cryptography. Furthermore, we focused our attention on analyzing hash functions and digital signatures, which complete the range of opportunities that asymmetric cryptography offers for key management, authentication, and data integrity.

Finally, we analyzed the main data structure that supports the blockchain, the Merkle tree, showing a concrete example of its implementation using the Python language.

Our journey continues in the next chapter, focusing on blockchain security assumptions and potential threats.

3
Blockchain Security Assumptions

In this chapter, we will focus on the security assumptions underlying blockchain technology and **distributed ledger technology (DLT),** examining in detail the advantages and disadvantages associated with each technological architecture.

After examining the characteristics of the decentralized model typical of blockchain and DLT, we will learn about the current threats to blockchain and DLT. We'll also discuss the potential future threats related to the spread of quantum computing, which represents a real risk not only for blockchain technologies but for all architectures that base their security on cryptography.

The topics we will cover in the chapter are the following:

- Centralized models versus decentralized models
- Advantages and disadvantages of blockchain
- Blockchain versus DLT
- Understanding transaction security
- Attacking a blockchain
- Understanding the quantum computing threat

Let's start by comparing the different centralized and decentralized architectural models.

Centralized models versus decentralized models

The first considerations regarding the security assumptions that characterize a blockchain must be conducted with reference to the architectural differences of blockchains, with respect to traditional application solutions. The comparison must, therefore, be made between two different application design models: a centralized model and a decentralized one, adopted in the development of applications.

Let's start with the first one, the centralized model, which is typical of the internet since its origins.

The centralized application model

Usually, an application developed according to a centralized model consists of an architecture with a central server (storing the applications, the database, the files, and so on) to which the client nodes connect in order to request the services offered by the deployed applications. It is the classic example of a client-server model, very widespread on the web, in which a central node acts as a server, making the services published on the server available to an unknown number of clients.

Despite its simplicity of design, this architecture immediately showed its limits, as the central node acting as a server turned out to be the weakest link, or rather, the single point of failure of the entire architecture. One of the most common attacks that can be conducted on a client-server architecture is a **Denial of Service** (**DoS**) attack, in which the attacker quickly saturates server resources by making a huge number of connection requests so that the server cannot serve new connection requests from legitimate clients.

The most common solution that is adopted to deal with DoS attacks consists of deploying redundant server resources. This is done by installing applications on multiple server machines, which can replace the central node in serving client connection requests when the central node is overloaded with requests.

However, this solution is insufficient to deal with **Distributed Denial of Service** (**DDoS**) attacks, in which the attacker, after obtaining control of an unknown number of client machines (by installing malware on them of the command and control type), performs the attack by ordering the *zombie* machines to send a large number of simultaneous connections to the server, thus saturating the redundant nodes as well.

As a matter of fact, in a centralized application model, the server assumes full control of the information published and made available to client nodes. Furthermore, if the resources published on the server are compromised (for example, following a data breach that modifies the data stored in the database), the entire reliability of the services published by the server is compromised.

We can, therefore, summarize the limits of the centralized application model as follows:

- As a single point of failure, the centralized model is more fragile and less stable.
- It is more difficult to protect against attacks that may affect data integrity and privacy preservation.
- The centralization of authority over published content may lead to trust issues.

In order to overcome these limits, the decentralized application model has recently grown in popularity.

The decentralized application model

The main feature of the decentralized model is, therefore, the absence of a central **master** node, which takes on all the responsibility of providing services to the client nodes, thus assuming full control of the reliability, integrity, and trustability of the published contents. This characteristic is typical of **peer-to-peer** (**P2P**) architectures (just think of applications such as BitTorrent, in which each node takes on the function of client and server).

Blockchain was designed to achieve the decentralization of transactions and trust, thus eliminating the need for a central authority that plays the role of intermediary in guaranteeing trust relationships. Unlike centralized applications, in a blockchain, trust is inherent to the consensus achieved by the network.

To understand the differences, just think of a typical example of a commercial transaction, such as buying an asset on an e-commerce website, and compare the same transaction performed within a blockchain. When purchasing on an e-commerce website, the trust in the transaction is imposed by the seller, acting as an intermediary between the producer of the item and the buyer.

In the case of the blockchain, the trust in the transaction is guaranteed by the network itself, without the need for third parties.

Therefore, with respect to the limits of the centralized model, the advantages deriving from the adoption of the decentralized model are the following:

- The absence of a single point of failure, guaranteeing greater stability and the robustness of the architecture
- Greater security and resistance to attacks
- A lack of the centralization of information control
- A guarantee of integrity and transparency in transactions
- Cost reduction due to the elimination of intermediaries in transactions

Obviously, the decentralized model is not without disadvantages. We will look at some of these disadvantages when we discuss the pros and cons of blockchain in the next section.

Advantages and disadvantages of blockchain

As a decentralized model, blockchain and other technologies that are inspired by it offer all the advantages seen in the preceding paragraphs, in addition to a series of specific advantages, which we will summarize here, together with the disadvantages.

Advantages of blockchain

Transaction immutability: Leveraging the hashing and encryption features we analyzed in `Chapter 2`, *Cryptography Essentials*, blockchain guarantees the immutability and non-repudiation of transactions. In other words, the blockchain ledger does not allow the deletion of existing transactions, and any changes made to them will result in new transactions that are added to existing ones, thus maintaining the continuity over time of their previous history.

Transaction redundancy: By virtue of the decentralized nature of blockchain, the transaction archive is replicated in every single node of the network. This feature prevents the loss of data in the event of some nodes being compromised. As such, blockchain can ensure a high level of fault tolerance.

Enhanced transparency and trust: To be validly inserted in the ledger, each transaction must be subjected to a validation process carried out by each node of the network. In this way, no transaction can be entered (or modified) into the blockchain without the network participants being aware of it.

In the same way, the counterparties of a transaction cannot deny having conducted a specific transaction between them, as the whole network can testify to the contrary, thus contributing to consolidating the trust that all participants place in each other.

Disadvantages of blockchain

Besides the advantages, some disadvantages and challenges of blockchain should not be ignored. Here, we indicate the main ones, some of which represent the flip side of the advantages we listed previously.

Scalability and performance issues: As a result of the fact that each node must validate and keep a copy of blockchain transactions, the performance of networks tends to worsen. With the increase in the number of participating nodes and the executed transactions, the overall scalability is negatively affected. Poor performance is also faced due to the limited computational power (including storage and network bandwidth) of each node.

Response times also deteriorate as the number of network nodes increase, due to the increase in latency.

Limited transaction volumes: Another problem is related to the limited number of transactions per second that can be managed by blockchain architectures, which in the case of the best implementations does not exceed the order of 1,000 per second, while in the case of Bitcoin, they reach approximately 7 transactions per second (this value is due to the Bitcoin protocol restricting block sizes to 1 MB).

There are the same considerations for Ethereum, which, although reaching around twice the number of transactions per second compared to Bitcoin, does not exceed 15 transactions per second.

Compared to the high volume of transactions that a traditional client-server application solution can handle, which averages in the order of a few tens of thousands of transactions per second, it immediately appears evident that the choice of technological solution based on blockchain is strongly limiting in certain business scenarios (such as financial asset trading, which involves the execution of transactions in real time).

Anonymity and confidentiality issues: While the fact of having a transparent transaction ledger ensures that no one can hide or change transactions without the permission of the other participants, on the other hand, it has a number of possible negative implications regarding the claims of anonymity and the privacy protection of participants in transactions.

Since the digital identities associated with the nodes participating in a blockchain do not necessarily correspond univocally to physical identities in the real world, this leads many to believe that it can be easy to remain anonymous in a blockchain, even if transactions are public.

Unlike what one might think, maintaining anonymity in a blockchain is extremely difficult. If even only some of the transaction counterparties fail to maintain an adequate level of anonymity, that may compromise the anonymity of all participants taking part in that same transaction.

In order to guarantee a high level of confidentiality, specific solutions have been designed (such as Zcash), if the protection of confidentiality constitutes an indispensable application requirement.

Issues in fixing errors: Likewise, the immutability of the ledger can prove to be a disadvantage in the presence of transaction errors. In the event of errors or bugs within transactions, which in blockchains such as Ethereum may also affect smart contracts (self-executing contracts), it is difficult to manage their correction by adopting the necessary fixes in time to avoid possible damage.

We have looked at the main advantages and disadvantages of blockchain in general; now, we must deal with other technologies that, although inspired by blockchain, must be kept distinct from it.

Blockchain versus DLT

The time has come to clarify the distinction between blockchain (that is, the technology supporting Bitcoin) and the other technological implementations that are inspired by it but are different in many non-secondary aspects.

These technologies are usually referred to as DLT, precisely so as not to confuse them with blockchain. DLTs fall into the more general category of distributed databases, which consist of databases whose archives are replicated on multiple nodes.

 It should be noted that not all distributed databases represent distributed ledgers, just as not all distributed ledgers constitute blockchains (we specifically use the term in lowercase to avoid confusion with Bitcoin's blockchain).

In distributed databases, in fact, the state of the archives is maintained consistently by the presence of an entity that plays the role of central authority. Unlike distributed databases, the distributed ledgers do not need a central authority, delegating to the nodes of the network the task of managing the synchronization of the state through the use of specific consensus-sharing mechanisms.

By their nature, blockchains are distributed ledgers implemented as chains of blocks linked together, which represent a set of transactions signed by using cryptographic functions, as we saw in `Chapter 2`, *Cryptography Essentials*. Even the different forms of access granting contribute to distinguishing between the various types of distributed ledgers.

In the case of permissionless DLTs, access to the ledger is granted to anyone, without the need for authentication; unlike permissioned DLTs, where access to the ledger is restricted to a limited circle of trusted counterparties.

From the preceding considerations, we can draw some conclusions about the opportunity to adopt technological solutions based on blockchains or DLTs. The technologies based on distributed ledgers are still largely experimental and, beyond their promises, they often do not stand up to comparison with more traditional solutions. It is therefore important to understand in which cases it is not advisable to rely on them, preferring instead to rely on more consolidated solutions.

As a matter of fact, blockchains and DLTs are highly inefficient, and before adopting them in production, it is necessary to ask whether it is really necessary to implement decentralized solutions to respond to our use cases.

These implementation differences also have important consequences in preserving transaction security, as we will see in the next section.

Understanding transaction security

Ensuring the security of online transactions has always been a problem for web applications. The traditional solutions adopted by e-commerce sites, as well as by remote banking sites, use the encryption of communications (for example, through the SSL/HTTPS protocol) established by users previously identified by personal authentication credentials. Encryption prevents the possibility of sensitive information (such as credit card numbers) relating to transactions being exposed to prying eyes but does not prevent the possibility of sensitive information leakage due to data breaches affecting the servers.

By leveraging these data breaches, it is possible for an attacker to exploit the user's sensitive data to conduct unauthorized transactions, in place of the unsuspecting user (identity theft). In the case of blockchain, by definition, transactions are public and transparent, to allow the nodes of the network to validate them, thus ensuring the immutability and non-repudiation of the transactions recorded in the ledger.

It should be emphasized that the fact that in a blockchain, transactions are public does not mean that confidential information relating to users is publicly disclosed. In fact, blockchain users can demonstrate their digital identity (and the ownership of assets exchanged in transactions) simply by signing transactions with their private key (which fulfills the same role as personal login credentials on traditional websites).

It is clear that it is the duty of individual users to protect and properly preserve their private keys since the loss of a private key could result in the loss of all their assets and funds recorded in the blockchain.

Securing private keys

The advantage of using private keys as the only personal credential needed to identify individual users and their assets on a blockchain is therefore balanced by the need to adequately protect these private keys. Private keys can be stored in special wallets, thus preventing their possible theft.

It must be kept in mind that the security measures adopted to protect private keys are more stringent than those adopted for traditional access credentials, precisely because of the fact that a third party (such as a bank or an e-commerce site owner) does not intervene in their management, therefore the responsibility for the security of private keys lies entirely with the user.

To adequately protect private keys, it is advisable to follow some best practices, such as the following:

- Storing multiple backup copies in different storage
- Preventing network access to storage containing backups
- Storing private keys in a paper wallet, which is a physical document

As the protection of private keys is often a burdensome task, many users often decide (mistakenly) to entrust the storage of their private keys to cryptocurrency exchange sites. Such sites can be subject to the same vulnerabilities already highlighted in the case of traditional web applications, as users' private keys are stored in publicly accessible servers, exposing them to possible theft, as in the cases of the Mt. Gox and Bitfinex security incidents.

Blockchain transaction weaknesses

The public nature of the transactions performed on a blockchain can be exploited by attackers to carry out different types of scams. The Mt. Gox incident of 2013 is an example of how it is possible to artificially raise the price of Bitcoins by implementing a sequence of fraudulent transactions that simulate a growing demand for Bitcoins on different cryptocurrency exchange sites.

Similarly, since the transactions recorded in the blockchain are immutable and irreversible, it is possible to exploit this feature to carry out scams against unaware users. An attacker may induce victims to spend their money in the form of Bitcoins to scam websites, thus removing the right for them to get their stolen money back.

Now let's see what the most common attacks that can be conducted against a blockchain are.

Attacking a blockchain

The methods of attack against blockchains are obviously different from those commonly used against traditional application solutions, as the vulnerabilities of the various architectures differ from each other.

In principle, blockchain-based technologies are usually immune to common attacks on traditional web applications. In other words, attacking a blockchain-based architecture adopting the typical attack strategies used to attack traditional architectures would not work, as the blockchain decentralized model makes these strategies mostly ineffective.

It should be borne in mind, however, that some specific blockchain implementations may still suffer from some form of centralization in some of their relevant components, including the consensus mechanism of the network. The preferred target by the attackers thus becomes the consensus mechanism; since each blockchain adopts its own specific consensus mechanism, the attack methods will also be different.

Let's now look at some concrete cases of possible attacks on blockchain-like architectures.

The Sybil attack

One of the classic attacks against peer-to-peer network architectures is the Sybil attack. The attack tries to impersonate the majority of the network nodes, even assuming multiple fake identities, in order to compromise the reliability of the whole network, along with the reliability and integrity of the transactions registered within the ledger.

In this way, whoever succeeds in controlling the majority of the nodes of the P2P network is, therefore, able to invalidate it by setting up illicit transactions (that is to say, contrary to the rules dictated by the network) at will. In one sense, the Sybil attack represents the negation of the blockchain philosophy, as it undermines the trust relationships that can be established within a network by undermining its reputation mechanisms. This form of attack was theorized for the first time in a paper entitled *The Sybil Attack* by John R. Douceur, Microsoft Research, and involves any large-scale, P2P systems that may face security issues from malicious nodes.

Therefore, the inner redundancy of the P2P network does not constitute a valid solution against this type of attack, since if a single entity of the network is able to assume multiple identities (thus controlling an important percentage of the network), it is able to undermine the redundancy itself.

It is possible to distinguish between two types of Sybil attacks:

- A direct Sybil attack, in which the malicious nodes exercise their influence directly on the victim nodes
- An indirect Sybil attack, in which the attack on victim nodes is brought indirectly by malicious nodes leveraging a compromised node that acts as an intermediary (the middle node) for the attacker

There are several ways to prevent a Sybil attack, such as the following:

- Verifying the identities associated with single nodes: this is the solution proposed by the aforementioned paper. It is about introducing a trusted entity that certifies the nodes' identities, acting as a logically centralized authority. Actually, validation can also be performed directly from the other previously verified nodes.
- Assigning different levels of reputation to the single nodes of the network, thus recognizing them with different levels of priority in achieving a network consensus.
- Introducing a fee for the creation of new identities, thus reducing the incentive to create fake identities.

In reality, not all types of blockchains are similarly vulnerable to a Sybil attack, and the differences also depend on the consensus mechanism adopted by the network.

In the case of Bitcoin's blockchain, the consensus mechanism is based on **Proof of Work (PoW)**, which requires considerable amounts of computational capacity in order to verify the authenticity of the individual blocks (and the corresponding transactions embedded in them) to be inserted into the blockchain. This computational power would be lost (with significant economic consequences) if the blocks were rejected because they were recognized as invalid.

Conversely, miner nodes receive a certain number of Bitcoins for each successfully mined block as a reward for the huge computational power they spent to ensure the integrity and reliability of the blocks (currently in Bitcoin, the reward is established as 12.5 Bitcoins).

This system as a whole represents an important economic incentive to prevent possible misconduct, and in fact, PoW has proved particularly effective in countering collusive conduct, such as that of Sybil-type attacks.

We'll now look at a particular type of Sybil attack, known as a majority attack.

The majority attack

Also known as a 51% attack, this is a particular type of Sybil attack that is achieved when the attacker controls 51% of the mining capacity, which is determined by the network's hash rate.

Controlling more than 50% of the hash rate means being able to control the consensus needed to create new blocks in the blockchain, as well as exercising control over the inclusion, exclusion, and ordering of the corresponding transactions.

The 51% attack allows the attacker to do the following:

- Slow down the inclusion of transactions awaiting confirmation
- Modify or replicate existing transactions by performing double-spending attacks
- Split the blockchain by forking it

However, the attacker is not able to insert invalid transactions (which would, in any case, be identified and discarded), nor to appropriate transactions relating to other accounts, or to prevent already validated transactions from being inserted in the blockchain.

The only economic advantage that could be achieved by a 51% attack would be to carry out double-spending attacks, but this advantage should be compared with the potentially high cost of such an attack, as we will see shortly.

Estimating the chances of a 51% attack

Although a 51% attack can, in principle, be carried out against general consensus mechanisms, it is usually directed toward those blockchain architectures that adopt the PoW as a consensus algorithm.

This means that, in theory, even Bitcoin's blockchain is susceptible to such an attack (as also mentioned in the Bitcoin whitepaper). However, this does not mean that an attack is actually feasible in practice: in the case of Bitcoin, in fact, a 51% attack is highly unlikely, as it is very difficult (and costly) for a single entity to gain control of this much of the total network.

The success of a 51% attack, in fact, depends on the attacker's ability to perform the forking of a longer chain, thus inducing other nodes to take part in it.

In theory, it would not be strictly necessary to reach exactly 51% of the network's hash rate to carry out an attack. In fact, the probability of success can be estimated on the basis of the proportion of the hash rate controlled by the attacker with respect to the network's hash rate, based on the number of confirmations requested by the blockchain in order to confirm transactions.

Assuming that **h** is the fraction of the hash rate controlled by the attacker, and **m** is the fraction of the remaining hash rate available to other nodes of the network, the probability of success, **P(s)**, of the attack is described by the following equation:

$$P(s) = (h/m)^c$$

Here, **c** represents the number of confirmations requested by the blockchain to confirm the transactions.

If the **c** parameter assumes the value **0** (no confirmation needed), the probability of success of the attack would be **1** (100%), regardless of the actual percentage of the hash rate controlled by the attacker.

For **c > 1**, the attack would have a 100% chance of success only if the attacker could control 51% of the total hash rate. Anyway, a chance of success lower than 100% can still be achieved by controlling a hash rate of less than 51%, according to the mathematical equation.

In other words, in the case of a lower percentage of the hash rate being controlled by the attacker, the chances of the attack's success would be reduced accordingly, but it may still remain concrete.

But there is an even more substantial reason that leads us to believe that a 51% attack is very unlikely: the cost necessary to actually achieve it.

Being able to obtain the control of 51% of the total network hash rate is in fact extremely expensive, especially when compared with the potential profit (very little, actually) that could be retrieved from double-spending operations (the only type of operations that can be concretely realized by leveraging a 51% attack).

The following table shows the cost estimates (expressed in dollars per hour) associated with the implementation of a 51% attack against some of the most common cryptocurrencies (estimated mean values relying on early 2018 observations):

Cryptocurrency	Hash rate (per second)	Estimated hourly cost
Bitcoin	35,600 PH/s	$750K
Ethereum	240 TH/s	$350K
Litecoin	330 TH/s	$50K
Monero	360 MH/s	$18K

From this table, it is clear that the possibility of creating a 51% attack is economically sustainable only with respect to those implementations that comprise a reduced number of nodes in the network.

In the case of the most widespread cryptocurrency blockchains (such as Bitcoin and Ethereum), the economic sustainability of a 51% attack is to be excluded (or the reasons underlying such an attack would be essentially political, rather than economic), given the low profits potentially achievable with a double-spending attack, which we will describe in the next section.

Double-spending attacks

In a double-spend attack, the attacker attempts to realize two (or more) different transactions using the same amount of money (it is like spending the same coin several times). This type of attack requires control of transactions on the blockchain, as we saw in the previous sections, since the attacker must be able to control the creation of new blocks at will in order to perform transaction reversing.

The problem with double-spending is a characteristic of digital currencies that are based on decentralized architectures. The probability of success lowers as the number of waiting block confirmations increases. In other words, counterparties that await a certain number of block confirmations before actually transferring assets ownership between them are less likely to be subjected to double-spending attacks.

Indeed, the only effective way to counter a double-spending attack is to wait for a certain number of block confirmations following the insertion of a transaction within a block. In this way, as the number of block confirmations increases, the chances of a transaction reversing are reduced, since the transaction lies **buried** deeper in the blockchain.

The number of block confirmations waiting varies according to the blockchain specification; this number is linked to features such as the mempool's size and the block computation time.

In the case of Bitcoin, the number of block confirmations suggested before actually transferring the assets is equal to at least 6 (since in Bitcoin, the confirmation of every single block occurs every 10 minutes, this means counterparties are advised to wait at least an hour before making the actual transfer of assets between them).

It is, therefore, a question of establishing the correct trade-off between the speed and security of the transactions carried out using cryptocurrencies.

The counterparties that accept the completion of transactions before having waited for the minimum suggested number of block confirmations, consequently, expose themselves to the risk of a double-spending attack.

Eclipse attacks

A typical attack that can be performed against a decentralized peer-to-peer network is an eclipse attack.

Unlike the attacks described previously, which targeted blockchain mechanisms (such as the consensus mechanism and block transactions), in the case of an Eclipse attack, the attacker's target is the network itself.

An Eclipse attack isolates some victim nodes from the rest of the peer-to-peer network, preventing them from communicating with the remaining nodes. Usually, the nodes of a peer-to-peer network make use of a special communication protocol (known as a gossip protocol) to establish connections between them, and to exchange information regarding the overall status of the network. In this way, the individual nodes are able to exchange relevant information without having to connect to a central node.

It is this feature that is used in an Eclipse attack.

Being connected directly to the victim node, the malicious nodes prevent it from receiving information from the other nodes, thus forcing the victim node to establish connections only with them. Here's an example of a victim node isolated by malicious nodes (depicted in red) from the rest of the P2P network:

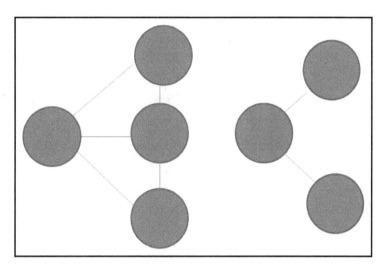

In this way, the updating of the victim node with the real global status of the network is inhibited by the fact that the victim node will believe only in the *truth* communicated to it by the attacker, being unable to communicate directly with the remaining trusted nodes of the network.

Not surprisingly, the predestined victims of an Eclipse attack are those nodes that play a special role within the network (in the case of Bitcoin's blockchain, they could be the miner nodes).

The first description of an Eclipse attack dates back to 2015 and is contained in a paper entitled *Eclipse Attacks on Bitcoin's Peer-to-Peer Network* by Ethan Heilman, Alison Kendler, Aviv Zohar, and Sharon Goldberg. The paper describes an attack against Bitcoin's blockchain, but it is clear that other forms of blockchains are also subject to this type of attack.

In the following section, we will describe an Eclipse attack against Bitcoin.

Eclipse attack on Bitcoin's blockchain

It must be premised that in a Bitcoin peer-to-peer network, there are limits to the number of connections that a node can establish with other peers. In particular, each Bitcoin's blockchain node can make a maximum of eight outgoing connections to other peers and can receive a maximum of 117 incoming connections from peers.

Furthermore, an attacker can exploit some Bitcoin vulnerabilities (such as the selection of IP addresses from the bucket with the latest timestamps, and the random removal of IP addresses from the bucket) to replace the IP addresses of the authentic nodes with the IP addresses of the malicious nodes.

By exploiting these limits and vulnerabilities, malicious nodes can force victim nodes to establish connections only with them.

The consequences of an Eclipse attack are also relevant to the upper layers of the blockchain.

An Eclipse attack can, in fact, constitute a means of compromising the security of the consensus mechanism, allowing the attacker to carry out a 51% attack even without actually controlling the majority of the network's hash rate, and to perform double-spending attacks on blockchain transactions even after awaiting a certain number of block confirmations.

In the case of a 51% attack, if the malicious node is a miner node, the attacker can carry out the attack without controlling 51% of the network's hash rate by preventing the remaining miners from obtaining the majority of the hash rate.

This can be achieved simply by eclipsing some victim miner nodes from the rest of the network, thus preventing miner nodes from reaching the majority of network resources requested to create blocks. By isolating the miner nodes from each other, the attacker increases the chances of forking and publishing a longer chain, with the help of victim miner nodes. This attack scenario could be realistic if the attacker leverages a botnet of zombie malicious nodes, as shown in the original paper *Eclipse Attacks on Bitcoin's Peer-to-Peer Network*, cited previously.

Now we come to double-spending attacks.

In the *Double-spending attack* section, we argued that this type of attack could be neutralized by waiting for a minimum number of block confirmations following a transaction.

By taking advantage of an Eclipse attack, an attacker could realize a double-spending attack in spite of waiting for a certain number of block confirmations. This result can be achieved by performing the eclipsing of some miner nodes, in addition to the victim node. Double-spending is thus performed by the attacker by forwarding a transaction to the eclipsed miner node, which in turn includes it in a new block. Then, the eclipsed miner node will show the updated blockchain with the confirmed transaction to the victim node.

At this point, the attacker creates another transaction using the same funds that were used for the previous one, forwarding the new transaction to the rest of the network for its confirmation, thus completing the double-spending attack.

After having analyzed possible attack types against the consensus mechanism, the transactions, and the peer-to-peer network of the blockchain, let's analyze some possible threats to the mining activity.

Mining pool security threats

The mining activity takes on a central role in all blockchains that use PoW as a consensus mechanism. Consequently, miner nodes have significant importance within such architectures (especially, the miner nodes with greater computational capacity) due to their higher capacity to contribute to the creation of blocks.

Since these nodes are also those that benefit the most from the mechanism of economic incentives underlying the mining activity, they tend to crowd out miner nodes with lower computational power.

To allow even nodes with less computational capacity to provide their own contribution to the mining activity, it is possible to combine these nodes in mining pools, at the same time, obtaining a more fair allocation of economic incentives.

The introduction of mining pools, however, has as its side effect the centralization of computational capacity, which contrasts with the decentralized philosophy of the blockchain, and therefore exposes the network to the security risks associated with such centralization.

As a result of this centralization of computational capacity, the creation of blocks within the blockchain risks being controlled entirely by mining pools, exposing the network to the threat of 51% attacks.

Selfish mining attacks

As we have seen, the activity of miners is of central importance within PoW-based blockchains. However, the system of economic incentives provided for their mining activity can induce miners to adopt selfish behaviors, which take the form of selfish mining attacks. In other words, some miners can decide to increase their rewards by keeping the blocks resulting from their mining activity private, rather than making them public.

The consequence of this selfish strategy implies that the chain of private blocks could become longer than the public blockchain, creating a competition between the chain constituted by public blocks (fed by the computational capacity of honest nodes) and the private blockchain (produced by selfish miners).

The competition between selfish miners can lead to unintended consequences, ranging from the invalidation of public blocks to the possibility of forks in the blockchain.

Such unintended consequences may, in turn, result in delays in achieving consensus within the network, which, as we have seen, exposes the network to risks such as double-spending attacks.

Forking attacks

A fork is usually the consequence of a dispute between nodes, regarding the agreed global state of the blockchain. These disagreements can be caused by malfunctions or by the presence of incompatible features in the software, but can also be intentionally caused to perform Sybil attacks, or as a result of a competition between selfish miners.

Whatever the case, a fork testifies to the presence of inconsistency within a blockchain, which can be exploited by attackers to undermine the network's trust. As a consequence of delays in reaching a consensus, it becomes difficult to manage fraudulent transactions.

So far, we have learned about some of the most common threats and attacks affecting blockchain's core characteristics, but a more subtle threat may be on the rise in the future: the quantum computing threat, which we will deal with in the next section.

Understanding the quantum computing threat

The threat posed by quantum computing is worth a separate section, given the efforts made by the IT industry to implement and commercialize a fully functioning quantum computing architecture in the near future.

In the research sector, quantum computing has, in fact, turned into a realistic opportunity; also in light of Google's recent announcement claiming that they have reached quantum supremacy, that is to say, they have managed to perform a calculation on their quantum computing platform that is not feasible with traditional computers.

In order to consciously assess whether quantum computing constitutes a real threat to the blockchain, and in general, for all those architectures that base their functionality on the use of the cryptographic primitives described in `Chapter 2`, *Cryptography Essentials*, we must first briefly introduce the fundamental concepts of quantum computing.

Quantum computing in a nutshell

The feature that distinguishes quantum computing architecture from traditional architecture (also known as von Neumann architecture) is the use of the effects of quantum mechanics (in particular, the superposition and entanglement of states) for computational purposes. The goal that quantum computing aims to achieve is to be able to introduce drastic reductions in execution times and in the resources needed to perform computational activities, by adopting a programming model that is substantially different from a traditional one.

In this sense, instead of the traditional bit, quantum computing introduces the qbit. Despite the similarities existing between the two information storage units, the qbit operating mechanism is substantially different from the traditional bit, since the qbit exploits the main properties of quantum mechanics. Through the superposition of states, the qbit is, in fact, able to represent more information within it at the same time. While the traditional bit can store within it only one of the possible values between 0 and 1, the qbit; on the contrary, is able to represent the superposition between 0 and 1, as such holding more information than its binary counterpart.

As a result of the superposition of states, quantum computers are able to perform calculations at a speed of several orders of magnitude higher than traditional computers.

Cryptography at stake

The greater computation speed that can be achieved by exploiting quantum computers has immediately represented a potential threat to the security of cryptographic algorithms, which are based precisely on the practical impossibility of solving some mathematical problems (such as factoring large integer numbers in prime factors) in a relatively short period of time.

As we know from `Chapter 2`, *Cryptography Essentials*, the reduction of prime factors of large integers (also known as the integer factorization problem) is considered a problem that cannot be immediately solved with current mathematical knowledge.

In fact, finding the prime factors of a large integer number adopting the **brute force** approach (essentially by trial and error) would require an estimated computational time in the order of thousands of years, if conducted by leveraging the computational power of traditional computers.

The difficulty of the factorization of large integer numbers is exactly what makes public-key cryptography algorithms (such as RSA) secure.

Similar considerations can be made for the discrete logarithm problem and the elliptic curve discrete logarithm problem, which constitute mathematically difficult problems to solve, and therefore guarantee the security of digital signatures and elliptical cryptography.

To understand how the difficulty in solving these mathematical problems can be overcome by the greater computational capacity made available by quantum computers, we need to introduce some concepts of computability theory.

Quantum versus traditional computability

Computability theory is the area of computer science research that deals with establishing what a computer can do.

When we talk about computers, we actually mean Turing machines. Turing machines are in fact the theoretical reference model used in computability theory. The Church-Turing thesis is applicable to Turing machines, which claims that any computable task can be computed by a Turing machine. The Church-Turing thesis, therefore, provides us with a criterion for determining what is computable and what is not, thus allowing us to understand what a computer can actually do.

Dealing with computability and decidability

It is important not to confuse the concepts of computability and decidability.

A problem is said to be decidable if there is an algorithm (that is, a predetermined sequence of steps) to solve it. For practical purposes, it is very important to know whether a problem is decidable or not (that is, whether or not an algorithm exists to solve it).

Although, in fact, a Turing machine is able to perform every computable task (based on the Church-Turing thesis), there are problems that cannot be solved by a Turing machine, such as knowing in advance whether the Turing machine will terminate the task that it is performing, or whether it will remain otherwise trapped in an infinite loop (this problem is also known as the halting problem).

Computational complexity

The concept of computability, therefore, regards only what a computer is able to do, without worrying about the resources needed to complete the task (such as the time and memory space required for the task to be executed).

The set of necessary computational resources is established by the computational complexity, which provides us with a practical evaluation criterion for computability. In other words, if a problem is theoretically computable but is so complex that it takes thousands of years to execute, it is, in fact, not computable in practice.

Usually, we define different classes of computational complexity, in which individual problems fall. For example, the computational complexity class P contains problems that can be solved by a Turing machine in polynomial time. These problems are therefore considered treatable and easily solved by a traditional computer.

A classic example of a problem that can be solved in polynomial time, and as such, falls into the P class, is the sum of two integers. Conversely, problems that cannot be solved by a Turing machine in polynomial time fall into the NP class.

Among these, there are precisely the mathematical problems posed as a prerequisite for the security of public-key cryptography algorithms.

Now let's look at the complexity classes for quantum computing.

Quantum computability and complexity

Just as we introduced the Turing machine concept for traditional computers, in the same way, we can define a theoretical model of the Turing machine for quantum computing, the **Quantum Turing machine** (QTM).

Likewise, we can introduce analogous definitions regarding the computability and complexity of QTMs.

Let's start with the Church-Turing thesis for quantum computing, which states that a QTM can be simulated by a Turing machine by executing a number of steps that are polynomial in the resources used by the QTM. This means that a quantum computing machine does not provide greater computational capacity than a traditional Turing machine, but greater efficiency in terms of resources used.

It is precisely for this reason that the solutions of mathematical problems, such as the integer factorization problem and the discrete logarithm problem, are tractable and can be solved in polynomial time on a QTM (while on a Turing machine, they would require execution times in the order of thousands of years).

However, this does not mean that some problems remain untreatable even by a QTM, as we will see in the next paragraph.

Quantum computing attack resistance

We have said that a QTM is able to solve problems in polynomial time that would otherwise be considered untreatable by a traditional Turing machine. This may lead some to erroneously believe that quantum computing is able to solve all kinds of computational problems, thus managing to break any cryptographic algorithm.

In fact, in solving hard mathematical problems (such as the traveling salesman problem or the shortest latex problem), quantum computers would not necessarily perform better than traditional computers. Where quantum computers show their best performance is in the computation of mathematical periodic functions.

Thus there are quantum algorithms, such as Shor's factoring algorithm, capable of breaking the cryptographic algorithms based on periodic functions (such as elliptical cryptography), while in the case of non-periodic functions, computational performance would not benefit from using a quantum computer.

Therefore, the use of non-periodic mathematical functions in the implementation of cryptographic algorithms would make these algorithms (and the architectures that are based on them) resistant to quantum computing attacks.

Summary

In this chapter, we looked at the security assumptions on which blockchain-based architectures are based, showing the specific vulnerabilities that can be exploited to conduct attacks against decentralized networks. We also covered the preferred targets of attackers who intend to take control of transactions on blockchains, aiming to compromise trust mechanisms. Finally, we analyzed the risks and threats to blockchains posed by quantum computing and discussed the most likely attack scenarios and possible countermeasures.

Our path continues now, on to understanding how blockchains achieve trust decentralization by leveraging P2P networking.

Further Reading

Anyone who wants to review the mathematics needed to understand the concepts of quantum computing can refer to *QC051 Math Prerequisites for Quantum Computing*, at `https://www.packtpub.com/programming/qc051-math-prerequisites-for-quantum-computing-video`.

2
Section 2: Architecting Blockchain Security

In this section, you will be introduced to the blockchain network topology role, which is all about ensuring that there's trust in blockchains and distributed ledger technology.

This section comprises the following chapters:

- Chapter 4, *Trustless Blockchain Networks*
- Chapter 5, *Securing Hyperledger Fabric*

4
Trustless Blockchain Networks

After having addressed the main features of the blockchain and outlined its main threats, we now deal with the mechanisms used to create trustless networks. Trustless networks are those networks that do not need to introduce a privileged node that guarantees trust within the entire network. On the contrary, trustless networks exploit the characteristics of decentralized networks, such as peer-to-peer (P2P) networks, to achieve trust in the network.

Over the course of this chapter, we will be using Bitcoin's blockchain as reference, since it represents the most successful case of blockchain, namely, Bitcoin's blockchain. We will also deal with the management of transactions within the blockchain, analyzing in detail the mechanisms for creating and synchronizing blocks.

We will conclude the chapter by analyzing the security aspects associated with cryptocurrencies, wallets, and the protection of private keys.

The topics analyzed in this chapter are as follows:

- Analyzing network discovery with P2P
- Block synchronization
- Transaction management
- Wallet key secure management

Let's start by analyzing the network discovery mechanisms used by P2P networks and, in particular, by blockchain.

Technical requirements

The code files of this chapter can be found on GitHub: `https://github.com/PacktPublishing/-Securing-Blockchain-Networks-like-Ethereum-and-Hyperledger-Fabric/tree/master/Chapter04`
Check out the following video to see the Code in Action: `https://bit.ly/2XnkMz5`

Network discovery with P2P

P2P networks constitute one of the most popular implementations of the decentralized network model. The peculiar characteristic of P2P networks is, in fact, the capability manifested by its peers to establish reciprocal connections between them without resorting to central entities, such as servers.

In fact, in a P2P network, each node assumes the role of client and server when it is appropriate (this is the reason why the nodes are also called **peers**). The main problem that arises in the implementation of a P2P network is represented by making the decentralized nature of the P2P network compatible with the topology and physical infrastructure of a public network such as the internet.

In the next section, we'll see how a P2P network can be deployed over the public internet.

Implementing a P2P network over the public internet

Unlike P2P networks, the topology of the public internet network is made up of a series of privileged nodes (so-called hubs) that act as concentrators for the network traffic. Therefore, the implementation of a P2P network using the public internet cannot immediately overlap on the existing physical topology.

It is therefore necessary to create a logical overlay that makes the two different network topologies compatible with one another. In a P2P network, the nodes can be connected together in a structured way following a predefined logic, or they can establish connections between them in a random and unstructured way.

The choice between these two options has advantages and disadvantages. If, on the one hand, it is easier to create an unstructured network, on the other, a structured network is able to exploit network resources more efficiently. In the same way, although an unstructured network is more robust thanks to the redundancy of the connections between the peers, however, it manifests latencies in the identification and search of resources. These latencies may be due to the possible overload of requests that need to be managed.

Let's now see how network discovery is implemented within a P2P network.

Implementing P2P network discovery

Network discovery within a P2P network takes on a particularly important function since, in the start up phase of a single node, there is no pre-existing network, but the network itself must be made up of the interaction between the various nodes.

Correct identification of the peers making up the network is therefore particularly important.

There are several ways to accomplish peer discovery in a P2P network. The most common are as follows:

- Hardcoding a list of a peers
- Deploying a resolution service (typically DNS) that maintains a list of peers

Let's now see how network discovery functions are implemented in Bitcoin's blockchain.

Network discovery in Bitcoin's blockchain

Whenever a new node intends to connect to the Bitcoin network, the network discovery process is started to allow the node to identify the other participating nodes in the blockchain.

By definition, blockchain is a decentralized network, and therefore there is no central server that can respond to the requests of the nodes. Hence, a mechanism for identifying the peers must be implemented at the startup of the node.

Peers are identified in two ways:

- Forwarding a DNS request by querying the DNS seeds
- By consulting the hardcoded list of IP addresses that is installed in the Bitcoin client

Let's now see how the two mechanisms work.

DNS seeds

DNS seeds are servers that implement a customized version of the well-known name resolution service **BIND (Berkeley Internet Name Daemon)** commonly used on the internet for the resolution of domain names. Unlike common internet DNS servers, DNS seeds contain lists of IP addresses associated with Bitcoin nodes.

The use of DNS seeds as a network discovery mechanism is managed within the Bitcoin client core by means of the `-dnsseed` parameter (whose default value is set to 1). DNS seeds are managed by members of the Bitcoin community, who manually enter IP addresses statically, as well as spread dynamic addresses.

Bitcoin hardcoded IP list

In addition to DNS seeds, Bitcoin clients can query the hardcoded list of Bitcoin nodes' IP addresses, which is downloaded together with the Bitcoin client installer.

This list contains the IP addresses of the stable Bitcoin nodes, also known as bootstrap nodes, precisely because of their function when starting Bitcoin clients.

Now, let's see how peer discovery occurs in Bitcoin.

Peer discovery in Bitcoin

At startup, each node must connect to at least one active peer on the network. After consulting the list of hardcoded IP addresses, or following the query of DNS seeds, the node is able to establish a connection with at least one other peer node. This connection is established through the TCP protocol by contacting port 8333 of the peer if the connection is established on the Bitcoin mainnet, or port 18333 in the case of the Bitcoin testnet. Once the connection is established, the handshake phase takes place, during which the nodes exchange the version message containing the updated information on the network (such as the version number, IP addresses, and the height of the blockchain).

At this point, with the information received, the node is able to easily identify the other peers currently active on the network and establish connections with them, in turn forwarding the information concerning itself to the rest of the network. The newly started node tries to establish up to 8 connections with the entry nodes; subsequently, the node can establish up to 125 concurrent TCP connections. Since the nodes within the network can deactivate in a non-pre-established way, it is important for peers to always have the updated list of active nodes.

To this end, Bitcoin provides an address propagation mechanism within the network, based on timestamps.

Bitcoin addresses

Within the Bitcoin network, participants in the transactions are uniquely identified by their respective Bitcoin addresses, which must not be confused with the IP addresses associated with the peer nodes of the network. A Bitcoin address is, in fact, the unique identifier of a counterparty participating in a transaction. Bitcoin addresses follow a specific encoding, being represented by the Base58 encoding associated with the hash of a public key.

An example of a Bitcoin address would look like
`mwog86wxZsWf6KGufzwA69xbvzE9TGZ5vA`. Each Bitcoin address is associated with a Bitcoin balance, the value of which can vary from Bitcoin fractions (expressed in units of measurement known as Satoshi, equal to 10^-8 Bitcoins) up to the maximum value comprising 21 million BTCs (corresponding to the number maximum of Bitcoins that it is theoretically possible to extract).

In the next section, we will see a detailed explanation of the relationship between Bitcoin addresses and cryptographic keys.

Bitcoin addresses and cryptographic keys

In `Chapter 2`, *Cryptography Essentials*, we examined the characteristics of the asymmetric cryptography keys; we will need these concepts now to better understand how Bitcoin ownership is verified within Bitcoin. Within Bitcoin, each user is associated with a public and private cryptographic key pair. The private key is also known as the secret key, as it must be protected from unauthorized access, and made inaccessible by other users. It is usually stored in a repository known as a wallet.

The public key, on the other hand, is publicly available to the rest of the network and is used to uniquely identify the user who is the legitimate owner. The generation of public-private key pairs in Bitcoin is carried out by means of elliptic cryptography. The Bitcoin's private key is represented by a 256-bit string, which can therefore assume a numeric value falling in the range between 1 and 2^{256}. To generate the key pair, you can use the `getnewaddress` and `dumpprivkey` utilities of the Bitcoin **command-line interface** (**CLI**).

To generate the keys, we will therefore run the following command:

```
bitcoin-cli getnewaddress
```

While, to extract the keys created previously, we will run the following command:

```
bitcoin-cli dumpprivkey
```

Having obtained the keys, we can better understand what Bitcoin addresses are.

As we have said, Bitcoin addresses unambiguously identify Bitcoin owners, and are created from public keys (in this way, they are inextricably associated with the corresponding secret keys).

Bitcoin addresses consist of three parts:

- Version prefix byte
- Hashed public key
- Checksum

The three parts are then chained together and encoded using Base58 encoding.

Let's first look at the characteristics of the individual parts, and then we'll see how to use them to obtain Base58 encoding.

The version prefix can take the following values:

- **1**: public key
- **2**: testnet hash script
- **3**: hash script
- **5**: private key
- **m**, **n**: testnet public key hash

To obtain the hash associated with the public key, we need to calculate the SHA256 and RIPEMD160 digests of the public key, based on the following formula:

```
hash = RIPEMD160( SHA256(pubkey) )
```

At this point, we are able to derive the third component of the Bitcoin address, namely, the checksum.

The checksum is obtained by concatenating the version prefix and the hash together, and applying the SHA256 algorithm twice to the string thus obtained (known as the **payload**). The initial 4 bytes must be extracted from the value thus obtained, which constitute the checksum.

The Bitcoin address is finally obtained by concatenating the checksum to the payload, and by encoding the character string thus obtained using Base58 encoding.

In addition to uniquely identifying Bitcoin owners, Bitcoin addresses can also be associated with transaction scripts, which we will see in the section dedicated to transaction management.

Analyzing blockchain network attacks

Based on what we have said so far regarding P2P networks, let's now analyze some of the most common attacks that can be launched against them, taking advantage of their constitutive characteristics, and having the blockchain as a reference.

Among the most common attacks that can be conducted against the blockchain are the following:

- DNS attacks
- DoS and DDoS attacks
- Eclipse attacks

We have already examined eclipse attacks in Chapter 3, *Blockchain Security Assumptions*, so we will now focus on other types of attacks, starting with DNS attacks.

DNS attacks

We have seen that at startup, each node must be able to locate the remaining nodes in the network. The network discovery phase, therefore, is particularly delicate and subject to attacks, such as DNS attacks.

Like all name resolution services, even blockchain's DNS-based network discovery can be subject to man-in-the-middle or cache poisoning attacks.

Following the injection of fake seeds into the list of seeds (DNS seeds poisoning), the attacker is able to isolate the peer nodes and redirect them to a fake blockchain under their control, which can lead to an eclipse attack as discussed in Chapter 3, *Blockchain Security Assumptions*.

Denial of Service attacks

The **Denial of Service (DoS)** attack consists of fraudulently exhausting the available resources of a service, thereby making it unavailable to legitimate users. Despite the decentralized nature of the blockchain, it is subject to DoS attacks, especially **Distributed Denial of Service (DDoS)** attacks.

In the blockchain domain, the DoS attack can take many different forms. It is known, for example, that in Bitcoin's blockchain, it is possible, on average, to validate a limited number (usually fewer than 10) of transactions per second. An attacker could exhaust this limited transaction validation capability after taking control of a sufficient number of wallets.

For example, the attacker could perform a certain number of transactions, each characterized by a limited amount of Bitcoins per single transaction, taking advantage of the stolen wallets' user credentials. Entering a large number of transactions in a short period of time, characterized moreover by small amounts in terms of Bitcoins exchanged, would congest the blockchain.

Such congestion would engage Blockchain in the creation of blocks for the validation of these large numbers of transactions.

As a consequence, legitimate users would experience a DoS in the validation of their transactions by the blockchain. Furthermore, following the DoS, the attacker could launch other attacks, such as double-spending attacks. Other forms of DoS may target the mempool (cache of unconfirmed transactions) in order to increase the expected mining fees.

In the next section, we will see some countermeasures to network attacks.

Possible countermeasures to network attacks

To prevent DNS-based attacks, various studies have focused on the possibility of introducing peer selection mechanisms aimed at maximizing the heterogeneity of routing paths, thereby limiting the possibility that the attacker can assume an advantageous position.

Other researchers have proposed the possibility of introducing anomaly detection mechanisms aimed at identifying anomalous behavior by peers, with the possibility of automatically isolating these nodes from the network.

As for DoS attacks, some changes to the block size have been proposed in order to be able to include more transactions within the blocks, or it has been proposed to introduce fees to increase the cost for the attacker intending to compromise the mempools.

Having analyzed the network discovery mechanisms, let's now analyze another central aspect of the blockchain: block synchronization.

Block synchronization

As we have seen in `Chapter 1`, *Introducing Blockchain Security and Attack Vectors*, the blockchain is nothing more than a list of blocks in which each block maintains a reference to the previous block. Within each block, in fact, the hash of the previous block is kept inside the `Prev_Hash` variable of the block header.

The hash stored within the `Prev_Hash` variable is obtained by calculating the `SHA256` algorithm on the block header of the previous block. In this way, an indissoluble chain of mutual references is formed, which guarantees that the data contained therein is immodifiable (in fact, it is sufficient to modify even one of the blocks to obtain totally different hashes).

It is therefore important that each node in the network is able to keep the local copy of the blockchain up to date by synchronizing the current status with the global status shared and validated by the rest of the network. This is exactly the job of the process known as block synchronization.

Let's now see how block synchronization occurs during node startup.

Synching blocks at node startup

When the node starts, it broadcasts a message to the rest of the network containing the value of the blockchain height, obtained from its local copy, which certifies the length of the blockchain local copy. The other peers of the network will reply to the message if their blockchain height value is greater (which corresponds to a longer blockchain), sending the inventory of information on the missing blocks to be added to the requesting node.

At this point, the node will be able to contact the remaining peers to obtain the updated blocks to be added to its local copy of the blockchain. As you can imagine from what we said so far, when starting a new node, the synchronization of the blockchain can be a very long process, as it is necessary to update the complete blockchain.

Once the first synchronization phase is complete, the node will simply synchronize the most recent blocks with each subsequent restart. In the event of a mismatch hash, that is, a mismatch existing between the hashes contained in the more recent blocks and the previously archived blocks, the node will nevertheless request the entire blockchain block sequence. After having fetched complete information on the individual blocks, the node is now able to independently verify the consistency of the blockchain.

To this end, the node must use the information saved within the block data structure, which we will examine in detail in the following section, referring to Bitcoin's blockchain.

Block data structure

The block data structure stores internally a series of information regarding both the block and the transactions it contains. As we know from Chapter 1, *Introducing Blockchain Security and Attack Vectors*, a block consists of a header and a body. Transactions are stored inside the body, while the header will contain the metadata relating to the block.

In the following table, we can see the fields contained in the block data structure:

Field	Description
Magic number	Always 0xD9B4BEF9
Block size	Size of the block
Block header	Block header
Transaction counter	Integer counter
Transactions	List of transactions

The block header, as we said, contains the metadata related to the block, and is represented by the following table:

Field	Description
Version	Block version
hashPrevBlock	256-bit hash of the previous block header
hashMerkleRoot	256-bit hash calculated on all transactions
Time	Current timestamp in seconds
Difficulty Bits	Current target
Nonce	32-bit number (starts at 0)

We note in particular the hashPrevBlock field, which contains the SHA256 hash referred to in the previous block, and the hashMerkleRoot field, which represents the hash of the Merkle tree containing the transactions, as we saw in Chapter 2, *Cryptography Essentials*.

The remaining fields of the block header, namely, the Time, Difficulty Bits, and Nonce fields, contain the information used by the consensus mechanism implemented within the blockchain to achieve network consent, as we will see in the following section.

Achieving consensus in a trustless network

As we know from Chapter 1, *Introducing Blockchain Security and Attack Vectors*, consensus within a trustless network is achieved by implementing a specific consensus algorithm. In the case of Bitcoin's blockchain, the consensus algorithm adopted is the **Proof of Work (PoW)**.

The PoW facilitates the attainment of consensus on the public ledger of the transactions by renouncing a central authority, relying instead on the contribution of the individual nodes of the network, who take on the following tasks:

- Adding data (namely transactions) to blocks to be inserted into the public ledger
- Validating each new block by checking its integrity, thereby ensuring that the block can be appended to the local blockchain
- Selecting the longest blockchain, representing the global state on which network consensus is achieved

The tasks performed by individual nodes must be coordinated with the work of the mining nodes, who are responsible for physically creating the blocks to be added to the blockchain, once all the previous nodes have been validated. It is the task of each node to verify that a block is valid, before inserting it in their local copy of the blockchain.

Block validation simply entails verifying the presence and integrity of the hash referred to in the previous block. The activities performed by the network nodes are all aimed at achieving consensus on the global status of the shared ledger; in the case of the PoW algorithm, this involves selecting the longest chain.

The length of the blockchain testifies to the computational effort (PoW) that it was necessary to employ in order to reach this dimension. Therefore, choosing the longest chain guarantees the attainment of trust within the network, as we saw in Chapter 1, *Introducing Blockchain Security and Attack Vectors*.

Since the work of the individual nodes takes place independently of the rest of the peers, conflicts between the blocks may occur on account of the differences in content inserted within them.

In the presence of different versions of the same block, each node will choose which of the two versions to add to the local copy of the blockchain (usually making this choice according to the order of arrival), before storing the discarded version in the mempool.

In this way, however, we will get different versions of blockchains, which can give rise to the phenomenon known as blockchain Fork. These forks are usually temporary, and are resolved as the network reaches consensus on the global state of the blockchain by selecting the longest chain.

The time has now come to explore blockchain more closely, using the `bloxplorer` Python library.

Exploring blockchain

In order to explore blockchain, we can recur to the Python `bloxplorer` library, which allows developers to make use of the Blockstream Esplora HTTP API (`https://github.com/Blockstream/esplora/blob/master/API.md`) through the Python interface.

As a prerequisite, the `bloxplorer` library requires the installation of Python version 3.6+.

To install the `bloxplorer` library, run the following command:

```
pip3 install bloxplorer
```

Readers can find full documentation at `https://valinsky.github.io/bloxplorer/`.

Let's now see some examples of the `bloxplorer` library in action.

Exploring Bitcoin addresses

By way of a first example of using the `bloxplorer` library, we will see how to obtain the information associated with a Bitcoin address.

In the following example, we will query the `testnet` Bitcoin:

```
from bloxplorer import bitcoin_testnet_explorer

btn_address =
bitcoin_testnet_explorer.addr.get('mwog86wxZsWf6KGufzwA69xbvzE9TGZ5vA')

print(btn_address.data)
```

Launching the script will give us the following output, printing the relevant information pertaining to the address we are investigating:

```
{ 'address': 'mwog86wxZsWf6KGufzwA69xbvzE9TGZ5vA', 'chain_stats': {
'funded_txo_count': 1, 'funded_txo_sum': 4809083, 'spent_txo_count': 0,
'spent_txo_sum': 0, 'tx_count': 1 }, 'mempool_stats':  {
'funded_txo_count': 0, 'funded_txo_sum': 0, 'spent_txo_count': 0,
'spent_txo_sum': 0, 'tx_count': 0 } }
```

Let's now explore a blockchain's blocks.

Exploring a blockchain's blocks

We'll now see an example script that fetches information pertaining to a blockchain's block:

```
from bloxplorer import bitcoin_testnet_explorer

blk_id = "00000000000001bcfbd6242711752c6d8eb15701eb19e410a39a45fa363926e9"

block = bitcoin_testnet_explorer.blocks.get(blk_id)

print("Block ID: ", block.data['id'])
print("Merkle tree root: ", block.data['merkle_root'])
print("Previous block hash: ", block.data['previousblockhash'])
print("Block timestamp: ", block.data['timestamp'])
```

Upon launching the script, this will be its outcome:

```
Block ID : 00000000000001bcfbd6242711752c6d8eb15701eb19e410a39a45fa363926e9
Merkle tree root :
55cdb5be1689027c81c9bf8731c05f955be49eece5639d99ad95ccbf9374cada
Previous block hash :
00000000000001decd01ced9b0b98f15ffb600f6abd27e0634809a90268b3765
Block timestamp : 1564789315
```

From the example, we can see how it is possible to trace back the blockchain by querying the block contained in the previous block hash field.

In this case, all we have to do is run the following statement iteratively:

```
prev_block =
bitcoin_testnet_explorer.blocks.get(block.data['previousblockhash'])
```

Then, we need to print the fields of interest that we wish to analyze.

Block vulnerabilities and attacks

Having examined block synchronization and explored the characteristics of the blockchain, we are now able to analyze the block vulnerabilities and possible attacks that target the blocks themselves. As we have seen, the creation and addition of blocks within the blockchain requires a series of concurrent activities by the nodes of the network.

As long as the blocks are not physically added to the blockchain, or definitively discarded, they can assume a state of inconsistency, such as the stale block. A block assumes stale block status in the event that, despite having been successfully mined, it is not, however, added to the blockchain.

A stale block normally occurs as a consequence of a race condition in the mining process, during which the miner's nodes are called to decide which is the next block to be inserted into the blockchain. However, the presence of a substantial number of stale blocks can be the symptom of a selfish mining attack, a type of attack that we analyzed in Chapter 3, *Blockchain Security Assumptions*.

We have also seen that there is the possibility of version conflicts between blocks; such conflicts can lead to temporary blockchain forks, but are also the result of block withholding and Finney attacks. In the case of the block withholding attack, the attacker's goal is to attack the mining pools by withholding valid blocks, and to create a fork following the attack, in order to receive the expected reward in both cases.

The Finney attack, on the other hand, is similar to the double-spending attack, in which a malicious miner node delays block propagation to achieve the double-spending of the funds involved in the transactions. To counter these forms of attacks, a series of solutions are being studied that will make it more burdensome for the attacker to pursue their goals by introducing economic disincentives.

Having analyzed the technical aspects related to block synchronization, we can now devote ourselves to transaction management.

Transaction management

The task of the distributed ledger is to record the transactions that have been validly concluded within the clockchain in an unmodifiable way. Before being entered into the blockchain, transactions must therefore be validated.

Pending their validation, the transactions are saved within the transaction mempool, which represents a set of unconfirmed transactions. Each node has the task of managing its own mempool transaction, waiting for the transactions to be validated.

You can query the list of unconfirmed transactions currently present in the blockchain by visiting the following link: `https://www.blockchain.com/btc/unconfirmed-transactions`. Anyone with access to the blockchain is able to view transactions.

Now, let's see in more detail what a transaction is.

Transactions in a nutshell

In Bitcoin, transactions represent each transfer of Bitcoins between users, identified by their corresponding Bitcoin public addresses. Each single transaction can contain multiple inputs and outputs, corresponding to the Bitcoins exchanged between the parties.

The amount in Bitcoin that can still be spent by a user is represented by the output that is not referenced in any of the transaction's inputs. This amount takes the name of unspent transaction output and is indicated conventionally by UTXO.

Each UTXO must be spent in its entirety, not being divisible. In the event that the amount of the UTXO is greater than the value of the transaction, the user will receive back the difference (less transaction fees), thereby giving rise to a new UTXO.

This mechanism is very reminiscent of what happens in ordinary transactions, in which we are returned change for the excessive payments made with traditional currency. Within a transaction, the value of the transaction outputs is stored in the `vout` variable. Symmetrically, a transaction input records the amount in Bitcoins associated with a previous transaction output.

In this way, all the transactions recorded inside the ledger constitute a chain.

Transaction verification

Transaction verification occurs through the use of particular scripts, known as locking/unlocking scripts. The scripting language used by Bitcoin is called Script, and takes the form of a stack-based language.

Script locking and unlocking is executed in sequence to verify the transaction, evaluating the values returned by the execution of the scripts that are saved on the stack.

Transaction scripts

Bitcoin provides two basic types of scripts, `scriptSig` and `scriptPubKey`. In addition to these, we have different types of scripts available, such as **Pay-to-PubKeyHash (P2PKH)** and **Pay-to-Script-Hash (P2SH)**.

The most frequently used type of script in Bitcoin is the **Pay-to-PubKeyHash (P2PKH)** script.

Let's now briefly examine the features of these scripts.

P2PKH scripts

In P2PKH scripts, a user who intends to transfer Bitcoins to another user will create a locking script associated with the recipient's public address. A transaction output will then be created within the transaction with a particular hash associated with it, the P2PKH. P2PKH is the public key hash associated with the recipient's public address.

In this way, only the recipient, who has the private key associated with the public address, is authorized to receive the amount contained in the transaction output, after verifying that the hash values calculated on the locking-unlocking scripts pair match.

P2SH scripts

Unlike P2PKH scripts, P2SH scripts use the hashes associated with the script itself, instead of the public address, to send the transaction output to the recipient. The funds are therefore expendable under the conditions provided in the script. To use these funds, it will therefore be sufficient to refer to the hash associated with the script. Since scripts have a lot in common with smart contracts, the topic will be explored in more depth in Chapter 6, *Decentralized Apps and Smart Contracts*.

Let's now see how transactions are added in blocks.

Adding transactions to blocks

It is the task of the miner nodes to aggregate the various transactions within a specific block. The miner node will then accumulate all the transactions received within its local mempool. Then, it will choose which of the transactions saved in the mempool to insert inside the single blocks.

We can now analyze an example of a transaction, using the `bloxplorer` Python library.

Exploring transactions

In the following example, we will print the transaction output associated with a specific transaction, identified by a specific transaction ID:

```
from bloxplorer import bitcoin_testnet_explorer

transaction_id =
'6d0139c3d0f529dda57496f1eabf0b32c9296c93b49b7a4965fa5ad91be4f216'

transaction = bitcoin_testnet_explorer.tx.get(transaction_id)

print("Transaction output: ", transaction.data['vout'])
```

Running the script returns the following output:

```
{
'scriptpubkey': 'a914e0725ef08b0046fd2df3c58d5fefc5580e1f59de87',
'scriptpubkey_asm': 'OP_HASH160 OP_PUSHBYTES_20
e0725ef08b0046fd2df3c58d5fefc5580e1f59de OP_EQUAL',
'scriptpubkey_type': 'p2sh',
'scriptpubkey_address': '2NDhzMt2D9ZxXapbuq567WGeWP7NuDN81cg',
'value': 39218600
}
```

From the output of the script, we can view both the value of the transaction output, along with the script associated with it, stored in raw format in the `scriptpubkey_asm` variable. The type of script used is P2SH, as can be verified by the `scriptpubkey_type` variable.

Let's now examine the final topic of this chapter – the safe management of wallet keys.

Wallet key secure management

One of the main problems associated with cryptocurrencies, such as Bitcoin and Ethereum, is that of being able to adequately protect users' private keys. As we know from Chapter 2, *Cryptography Essentials*, the knowledge of the public key does not constitute a security issue, as it is made available to anyone interested in contacting the public key holder.

In the case of the private key, instead, it is important to guarantee its maximum confidentiality: anyone who manages to gain possession of the private key automatically becomes able to use the funds contained in the transactions referable to it, on behalf of the legitimate owner.

By knowing the private key, in fact, anyone is able to view a user's account balance, querying the transactions associated with the account and recorded within the blockchain. The commonly adopted method for managing private keys is the use of wallets.

Let's see what these are.

Introducing wallets

Wallets are software or hardware devices specializing in the conservation of private keys associated with a specific user. Despite what is commonly believed, cryptocurrency wallets do not actually contain cryptocurrencies (such as Bitcoins), but only the keys and public addresses associated with the user. In the case of Bitcoin wallets, they contain only the user's keys, since knowledge of the keys is sufficient to manage the Bitcoins associated with those keys.

As we have seen in the previous paragraph, the funds are actually contained within the transaction outputs, and the user can claim ownership of these funds simply by signing the transactions with his own private key. Inside a wallet, it is possible to keep an indefinite number of keys.

Depending on the key generation mode, the wallets are divided into deterministic and non-deterministic, as we will see in the following sections.

Types of wallets

There are several different types of wallets. The first distinction to be made is between deterministic and non-deterministic wallets, a difference that is based on the existence, or otherwise, of existing relationships between the keys.

In the following sections, we will demonstrate the difference between deterministic and non-deterministic wallets.

Deterministic wallets

In deterministic wallets, the keys are generated from a master key. Therefore, the keys are linked together and can be recreated if necessary using the same master key, which then acts as a seed.

Non-deterministic wallets

In the case of non-deterministic wallets, the keys are randomly generated and, as such, they hold no relationship between them.

The greater security of the keys thus generated does constitute a disadvantage, however, from the point of view of their management. The keys, in fact, need to be backed up individually in order to prevent their loss, since they cannot be recreated once lost. Next to these two main types of wallets, there are others that differ in the way they manage and store the keys.

Let's look at the main types.

Paper wallets

Paper wallets are nothing more than the printing on paper of the public/private key pair, in QR code or phrases format. The purpose of the paper wallets essentially entails removing the secret keys from electronic devices (computers, laptops, tablets, and so on), which can be subject to remote attacks, by printing them on paper without the need for additional backup media.

If necessary, the keys can be entered by reading the corresponding QR codes.

Brain wallet

By using a brain wallet, it is possible to generate the public/private key pair from a passphrase that is simple for the user to remember, but difficult for the attacker to find, since the passphrase is **archived** exclusively in the user's mind.

Having introduced wallets, we now see the possible vulnerabilities that can afflict the secret keys and their management, identifying the possible countermeasures to the most common attacks.

In the next section, we will cover some of the most common wallet vulnerabilities.

Wallet vulnerabilities

Just as it is possible for keys to be stolen by an attacker, even the wallets containing the keys can be stolen as well. Therefore, wallets must be adequately protected to prevent their theft, or the compromising thereof. In the same way, wallets could be compromised by the action of viruses and malware of various kinds, or be subject to data leakage following the compromising of the servers on which they are installed.

This possibility is becoming increasingly likely, given the high diffusion of the services of online management of the wallet keys. Equally important, in the case of open source software such as Bitcoin and Ethereum, is to keep the versions of the installed software constantly updated.

Keeping software updated is important in order to avoid being exposed to bugs or vulnerabilities that may affect older versions. Just as it is important to download the installation software from reliable sites (with the source code being freely available), an attacker could pack a modified version of the source code, thereby injecting malicious code).

Having examined the main vulnerabilities that can afflict wallets, in the next section, we will look at some of the possible countermeasures.

Securing Bitcoin wallets

With the installation of the Bitcoin client software, the user obtains a wallet to manage their keys. However, it should be borne in mind that Bitcoin, by default, does not protect wallets with encryption; an attacker could therefore discover the user's credentials, as well as identify their transactions.

Similarly, the installation of the Bitcoin client must be carried out on a host adequately protected from possible malware attacks or external intrusions.

In the next section, we will learn how to secure online wallets.

Securing online wallets

Given the level of complexity associated with the adequate protection of wallets, it could be tempting to delegate the management of wallets and their security to third parties. To this end, numerous services are now available online, dedicated to the management of wallets. However, not all online services are created equal, nor are the security levels offered identical.

The user must therefore ascertain how the security of the keys is managed by the services offered by third parties. Some store the secret keys on their servers, having encrypted them beforehand. Others instead still keep the security keys on the client installation of the user, or even within the user's browser. In these cases, although users have delegated the management of their private keys to third parties, they are still exposed to the same types of compromises as if managing keys on their own.

In the same way, delegating the management of private keys to third parties implies a delegation of trust to unknown subjects, who can change behavior over time.

In the Bitcoin context, a type of wallet known as cold storage is spreading, through which it is possible to store Bitcoins offline, without keeping private keys online. Through cold storage, most of the consistency of Bitcoins is not kept online. The number of Bitcoins kept online is limited to what is strictly necessary to cover advance withdrawals.

In the next section, we'll learn how to secure paper wallets.

Securing paper wallets

We conclude our discussion by briefly considering the security measures necessary to protect paper wallets. As we said, paper wallets were introduced as an alternative to the digital archiving of private keys. The basic assumption is that paper wallets are, by definition, not subject to cyber attacks or malfunctions, as in the case of digital devices.

However, paper wallets are subject to all types of compromise typical of analogue documents (in the first place, the possibility of being lost, or deteriorating over time). In the same way, QR codes can also be subject to data leakage due to compromised digital acquisition tools, or websites that do not adequately preserve the confidentiality of user information.

Summary

In this chapter, we have dealt with various topics concerning the functioning of the blockchain, making particular reference to Bitcoin. We learned the features and vulnerabilities connected with network discovery mechanisms within trustless networks implemented through P2P protocols, and we focused, in particular, on the characteristics of block synchronization and blockchain transaction management, analyzing the vulnerabilities and possible threats to their integrity. The chapter concluded with the management of the security of the private keys stored inside the wallet keys.

We are now ready to analyze the architectural features and safety aspects of one of the most popular DLTs, namely, Hyperledger Fabric, which will be the topic of the next chapter.

Securing Hyperledger Fabric

5

In this chapter, we will learn about Hyperledger Fabric, one of the most well known industrial examples of **distributed ledger technology** (**DLT**). Although DLT solutions are inspired by blockchain, they nonetheless show peculiar and distinctive characteristics. We will, therefore, analyze the differences between blockchain and DLTs, examining the pros and cons of these technologies. After introducing the Hyperledger architecture, we will analyze the security aspects related to the digital identities associated with the members participating in the DLT, and we will examine the security of chaincode, the equivalent of smart contracts in Hyperledger. Finally, we will learn how to protect Hyperledger from security and privacy threats by using the product's features.

The topics covered in the chapter are listed here:

- Permissioned blockchains and DLTs
- Getting to know Hyperledger Fabric
- Hyperledger strong identities
- Hyperledger chaincode security
- Protecting against common threats with Hyperledger

Let's start by analyzing the characteristics of permissioned blockchains and DLTs.

Permissioned blockchains and DLTs

As anticipated in Chapter 1, *Introducing Blockchain Security and Attack Vectors*, when we speak generically of blockchain, we actually refer to differing types of technologies united by the fact of storing transaction information within a shared ledger. However, these differences take on significant importance, both in terms of implementation and security.

Therefore, it is important to explore the different characteristics of blockchain-based technologies, with particular regard to public and private (also known as permissioned) blockchains. This will allow us to fully understand the characteristics of Hyperledger Fabric, which represents one of the most popular permissioned blockchain implementations.

So, let's first clarify the distinction between public and private blockchains.

Public versus private blockchains

Public (also known as permissionless) blockchains are an example of a completely decentralized distributed ledger, in which an indeterminate number of members can freely participate without restrictions, equally contributing to the achievement of trust within the network. The most successful example of a public blockchain is certainly Bitcoin's blockchain. Bitcoin's success has shown how it is possible to reach consensus on transactions without the need for a central authority to verify, confirm, and guarantee the reliability of transactions.

One of the main disadvantages of public blockchains, however, is that as the size of the blockchain grows, transaction verification and confirmation operations become progressively more complex, slow, and inefficient. Complexity and inefficiency are also determined by the specific consensus algorithm adopted, which in the case of Bitcoin is the **Proof of Work** (**PoW**). Consensus algorithms tend to constitute a bottleneck in the number of transactions that can be verified and validated by the members of a network. The average of the transactions that can be verified and validated in Bitcoin's blockchain is in fact around 10-15 transactions per second.

PoW also means an increasing computational load as the size of the blockchain grows, with evident impacts in terms of the greater energy resources that are necessary to perform these operations. These disadvantages have led to the adoption of alternative blockchain models, the so-called private or permissioned blockchains. A private blockchain is characterized by the fact that there is an organization that establishes the rules of operation of the blockchain, decides who can take part in the network, and determines what type of operations can be carried out by the participants. In some sectors, such as the financial sector, it is possible for there to be multiple institutions interested in organizing their own private blockchains; in this case, the blockchain model used is that of the consortium (federated) blockchain.

Private and consortium blockchains are also called **permissioned blockchains**. Within a private blockchain, different members assume different levels of responsibility. For this purpose, unlike in public blockchains, in which members can freely participate without the need for identification, in the case of private blockchains, participants are identified in advance to guarantee the interaction between known and trusted counterparts. Therefore, since private blockchains represent a special case of permissioned blockchains, and since they are managed by an organization within a specific trust domain, they have access control procedures to limit access to the network to only trusted counterparties. The organization managing the rules and procedures for accessing the network will consequently assign predefined roles to the members of the network, with different privileges.

In the next section, we will delve deeper into permissioned blockchains access rights.

Permissioned blockchains access rights

Blockchains models can, therefore, be distinguished based on the privileges associated with members.

In general, participants in a blockchain can do the following:

- Access data and transactions (read access),
- Enter their own transactions (write access),
- Update the status of the blockchain by creating new blocks (update access),

Based on these access rights, it is possible to distinguish the different blockchains models as follows:

- **Permissionless (public) blockchains**: Any members of the network can perform read, write, and update operations without restrictions.
- **Permissioned (private) blockchains**: Read, write, and update operations are allowed and assigned only to certain members of the network, based on the roles identified by the organization that manages the blockchain.

Due to the limitation of the operations allowed to members, permissioned blockchains are not considered by purists (especially by the Bitcoin community) to be authentic blockchains, but DLTs.

DLTs as permissioned blockchains

Permissioned blockchains are traced back to DLTs as they mainly meet the needs of those organizations interested in managing a shared ledger exclusively internally. In practice, although constituting decentralized ledgers, permissioned blockchains distinguish the nodes of the network based on their roles and on the basis of the privileges assigned to them.

Recall that in permissionless (public) blockchains, no distinctions are made between nodes. Furthermore, in public blockchains, the transaction ledger is practically unchangeable, while in permissioned blockchains the possibility of modifying transactions is far from excluded. Usually, permissioned blockchains use a consensus algorithm different from PoW, which is commonly used in public blockchains.

As we know, the PoW consensus algorithm guarantees the integrity and immutability of the transaction ledger. This, however, comes at the cost of an increase in the computational load and reduced performance in terms of the number of transactions per second. The consensus algorithm usually adopted in the permissioned blockchains is the **Practical Byzantine Fault-Tolerant (PBFT)** algorithm, which offers better results in terms of performance, while ensuring an adequate level of fault tolerance.

To fully understand the implications of choosing a different consensus algorithm, we need to examine how consensus is achieved within permissioned blockchains.

Consensus in permissioned blockchains

As we saw in Chapter 1, *Introducing Blockchain Security and Attack Vectors*, the purpose of the consensus mechanism is to allow blockchain nodes to reach an agreement (consensus) on the current state of transactions. The consensus mechanism must also be fault tolerant; that is to say, it must be able to function even in the presence of malfunctioning or dishonest (also known as Byzantine) nodes. This requirement takes us back to the Byzantine failure problem, this time in the context of permissioned blockchains. As we said, in permissioned blockchains, we prefer to adopt an alternative consensus algorithm to PoW, to improve performance and reduce energy impact.

However, it remains to be seen at what cost, in terms of the resilience, integrity, and reliability of transactions, the replacement of the PoW occurs. The requirement of resilience for the problem of the Byzantine generals is reduced to determining what the correct proportion of legitimate nodes in the network is. This proportion is compared to the overall number of unreliable nodes. In fact, it is necessary to preserve a consistent proportion of legitimate nodes, to guarantee the correct functioning of the consensus algorithm. In the presence of n independent nodes, we must, therefore, determine the value $f < n / k$ (where k is an integer greater than 2), beyond which we cannot tolerate fault nodes, under penalty of a lack of reliability in the consensus mechanism.

In the case of the PBFT algorithm, commonly adopted in the implementations of the most popular permissioned blockchains, it is demonstrated that $k = 3$. This means that PBFT can tolerate a maximum value of $f = n / 3$ total fault nodes and still continue operating regularly and guaranteeing the consistency of the blockchain. The blockchain consistency translates into the absence of forks; the PBFT algorithm is therefore able to guarantee blockchain consistency, at the expense of availability.

To better understand the reasons behind this trade-off, we will introduce the CAP theorem in the next section.

Assessing availability and consistency with the CAP theorem

Originally postulated by Eric Brewer, the CAP theorem states that in a distributed archive, it is possible to guarantee at most two of the following properties:

- Consistency (C)
- Availability (A)
- Partition tolerance (P)

Based on the properties that can be respected simultaneously, distributed archives can be denoted as **AP**, **CA**, or **CP**.

Since blockchains must be able to tolerate partitions in order to function, the **CA** case is not contemplated, and the possible combinations are reduced to only two: **AP** and **CP**.

The preceding properties mean the following in the case of blockchain:

- **Consistency**: The absence of forks in the transaction ledger.
- **Availability**: The ledger and the transactions recorded in it are always available to all nodes.
- **Partition tolerance**: The network continues to function regularly even in the presence of delayed or dropped blocks.

With this, we are now able to compare the different consensus algorithms, based on the CAP theorem. In the case of PoW, we know that it does not guarantee consistency, as the presence of forks in the blockchain is always possible. Although the probability that these forks may persist over time decreases exponentially, with the addition of new blocks to the blockchain, the fact remains that the consensus mechanism implemented by the PoW is essentially probabilistic: the value of 100% consistency is achieved only asymptotically.

Therefore, in public blockchains such as Bitcoin, consistency is pursued through economic incentives, consisting of the rewards awarded to miners. In the case of PBFT, on the other hand, consistency is guaranteed by the consensus algorithm itself, provided that there are less than **1/3** of fault nodes with respect to the total number of nodes in the network. However, in PBFT, consistency is achieved at the expense of availability, based on the CAP theorem. Therefore, according to the CAP theorem, PBFT can be denoted as **CP** and PoW as **AP**.

Well, we are now able to analyze one of the most popular permissioned blockchains, Hyperledger Fabric.

Getting to know Hyperledger Fabric

Hyperledger Fabric is a permissioned blockchain managed by a consortium of companies. The project has been hosted and promoted by the Linux Foundation since December 2015, since the Linux Foundation together with 30 sponsoring companies (including IBM) decided to create an enterprise-class open source blockchain. Other major companies of the caliber of Intel, Accenture, and Huawei have subsequently joined the project, and their number currently exceeds 250 members.

Hyperledger Fabric is designed to provide high flexibility and extensibility, both at an architectural and application level. The modular architecture extends to the consensus mechanism, thus allowing specific consensus algorithms to be adopted on the basis of the different use cases, simply by choosing the most suitable component to implement the consensus mechanism of choice. The management of membership policies is also implemented in a modular form, thus allowing the adoption of custom identity management components.

Like many other blockchains, Hyperledger Fabric also supports the execution of smart contracts, which in this case takes the name of chaincode. Unlike other implementations, which require specific languages for the development of smart contracts, standard programming languages can be used in Hyperledger to develop smart contracts. In addition to flexibility and modularity, Hyperledger Fabric aims to achieve high levels of confidentiality, scalability, and resilience that are essential to meeting enterprise-class needs. Among the industrial sectors in which Hyperledger is currently employed, there are logistics and the financial sector, with more being added gradually.

Let's take a closer look at the architecture of Hyperledger Fabric in the next section.

Hyperledger Fabric architecture

Being a permissioned blockchain, in Hyperledger Fabric, all participating nodes are identified and take on a specific role within the network.

These are the roles that the nodes can assume:

- **Clients**: These propose transactions for execution.
- **Orderers**: These constitute the ordering service, which is the service that maintains the overall order of transactions within the ledger.
- **Peers**: These execute and validate the transactions proposed by the clients; they also have the task of maintaining the transaction ledger.

The architecture of Hyperledger Fabric is functional to the execute-order-validate paradigm, which differs from the classic order-execute paradigm commonly adopted by traditional blockchains, as we will see shortly.

The execute-order-validate paradigm divides the transaction flow into three different moments:

- Execution of the transaction and verification of its outcome
- Transaction ordering via a consensus mechanism
- Transaction validation and ledger update

This division of the transaction flow means that transactions are executed before the consensus is reached on their order. This division allows Hyperledger Fabric to perform transactions in parallel, and to update the transaction ledger only after reaching consensus on the total order to be assigned to the transactions as a whole, in a deterministic manner.

The ordering of the updates to be carried out on the ledger is then delegated to the consensus component, which acts independently with respect to the execution of the transactions. This guarantees the modularity of the consensus mechanism and the possibility of adapting it to the different trust domains. The result obtained through the execute-order-validate paradigm is to have a scalable architecture, which is also adaptable to different trust models.

The implementation of the scalable and flexible architecture of Hyperledger Fabric is entrusted to the following components, which can be implemented using tools already available as open source:

- **Membership Service Provider** (**MSP**): Assigns the roles and manages the identities of the individual nodes, preserving the characteristics of the permissioned blockchain.
- **Ordering service**: This spreads the status updates of the ledger to the nodes and maintains the overall order of the transactions through the consensus component; among the tools usually used to implement the ordering service are Apache Kafka and ZooKeeper.
- **Ledger maintenance**: The peer nodes keep the ledger of the transactions in the form of a blockchain; they also keep the most recent updates of the ledger in key-value format, by means of archiving tools such as Apache CouchDB.

To these main components is added the smart contract execution environment, in which smart contracts are executed without having direct access to the ledger.

Smart contracts follow the specific application model established by Hyperledger Fabric.

Hyperledger Fabric application model

Within Hyperledger Fabric, transactions between members of the permissioned blockchain take the form of smart contracts. As we have said, unlike the case for other blockchains, in Hyperledger Fabric, smart contracts can be developed using common programming languages, such as Java, Python, and Node.js. Smart contracts in Hyperledger Fabric are called chaincodes, and are executed in the execution phase. Since the chaincodes can be developed by untrusted parties, to be executed they must be associated with endorsement policies. Most of the time, they take the form of libraries that validate the instructions and transactions within chaincodes.

Now that we've introduced the architecture of Hyperledger Fabric, let's see now what the main differences it has with traditional blockchains are.

Hyperledger Fabric versus other blockchains

The main difference is the non-standard paradigm adopted by Hyperledger Fabric to carry out transactions. Traditional blockchains, in fact, follow the order-execute paradigm, while Hyperledger Fabric, as we have seen, introduces the execute-order-validate paradigm.

The question that arises now is this: *why must Hyperledger Fabric introduce this new paradigm?*

To understand why, we need to analyze the traditional transaction flow according to the order-execute paradigm, which requires that transactions must first be ordered through a consensus algorithm, and then executed.

In a public blockchain, where the consensus mechanism adopted is based on PoW, the transaction flow would be as follows:

- The node inserts the transaction into a block.
- The node must solve the cryptographic challenge to achieve PoW.
- If it succeeds, the node can forward the block to the rest of the network for validation.
- Each node that receives the block proceeds to the sequential validation of the transactions contained in the block.

Although simple and straightforward, the order-execute paradigm is not a good fit for permissioned blockchains.

The reasons are essentially attributable to the following aspects:

- **Sequential transactions validation**: All peer nodes must sequentially validate all transactions within the block; this drastically reduces the number of blocks (and therefore of transactions) that can be added to the blockchain for a period of time.
- **Smart contracts as Turing-complete programs**: The execution of smart contracts could further aggravate this inefficiency, exposing the blockchain to **Denial of Service (DoS)** attacks: according to the Turing machine halting problem, there is no algorithm that allows us to identify in advance whether an instruction contained in a smart contract will perform an infinite loop with no possibility of stopping.
- **Transactions confidentiality**: In many cases, the adoption of a permissioned blockchain is dictated by confidentiality requirements, which impose restrictions on access to information relating to transactions, which do not reconcile with the need for the order-execute paradigm to allow each node to validate individual transactions.
- **Pluggable consensus mechanism**: Unlike traditional blockchains, in which the consensus mechanism is predefined and embedded within the implementation, in the case of Hyperledger Fabric, there is the option to choose the component that implements the consensus mechanism that best suits the needs of the trust model that the organization is willing to create.

These are the main reasons that led the Hyperledger Fabric designers to introduce the new execute-order-validate paradigm for managing the transaction flow.

Let's now see in more detail what the transaction flow of Hyperledger Fabric consists of.

Hyperledger transaction flow

Essentially, the transaction flow in Hyperledger Fabric is divided into three phases, corresponding to the execute-order-validate paradigm:

- The execution phase
- The ordering phase
- The validation phase

In the following sections, we will see the characteristics of the single phases.

Execution phase

In the execution phase, client nodes send their transaction proposals for execution. The transaction proposals take the form of chaincodes (smart contracts) and refer to specific endorsement policies. The transaction proposals contain references to the identity of the client node, which also signs them.

The execution of the transaction proposal is emulated inside an isolated container (typically, a dedicated Docker container), by an endorser process that applies the endorsement policies referenced by the transaction proposal. Being executed in an isolated container, the chaincode does not have direct access to the state of the ledger.

Following the emulation, and in compliance with the endorsement policies, the client node receives the endorsement, which is represented by a cryptographically signed message and is necessary for the client node to satisfy the endorsement policies. Once the endorsement policies are met, the client node creates the transaction and forwards it to the ordering service. As we have seen, the execution of the transaction before the ordering phase is essential to prevent unpredictable (and potentially harmful) behavior of the instructions contained in chaincodes.

Ordering phase

Once the necessary endorsements are obtained, the client node creates the transaction containing the chaincode instructions (transaction payload), the metadata, and the endorsements received, and forwards it to the ordering service. The task of the ordering service is to define the overall order of all transactions within the network.

Since Hyperledger Fabric allows you to combine multiple blockchains into the same ordering service, each separate blockchain is identified as a separate channel, together with its member nodes. Each channel, therefore, has a total order of transactions, which is distinct from other channels. The ordering service groups the transactions within the blocks and ensures that the blocks are fully ordered.

Since the ordering service does not maintain the state of the blockchain, nor does it proceed with the validation of transactions, Hyperledger Fabric can manage the consensus mechanism in a modular way. Once the blocks have been ordered, they are forwarded to the peer nodes for validation.

Validation phase

In the validation phase, the peer nodes verify compliance with the endorsement policies; if there is non-compliance, they mark the transaction as invalid and cancel its effects. A conflict check of all the transactions contained in the block is also carried out. For each transaction, the version of the keys is compared with the version stored in the node's local ledger.

As a final result of the validation phase, the block is added to the peer node's locally stored ledger, and the status of the blockchain is updated accordingly. All recent status updates are then stored in the key-value store.

In the next section, we will deal with Hyperledger strong identities.

Hyperledger strong identities

Of central importance in the permissioned blockchain model adopted by Hyperledger Fabric is the management of the digital identities of the members of the network. This ensures not only security but trust in transactions between trusted counterparties. In Hyperledger Fabric, the creation, maintenance, and revocation of digital identities is entrusted to a specific component, known as the **Membership Service Provider** (**MSP**). The MSP component manages digital identities in the form of cryptographically signed certificates. In Hyperledger Fabric, there is a default MSP, known as Fabric CA, which has the task of issuing certificates in X.509 format to be associated with members authorized to participate in the network.

But before we find out about the details of identity management, we need to focus on how to carefully design our network of trusted counterparts.

Designing a Hyperledger Fabric network

Since it's a permissioned blockchain, access to Hyperledger Fabric is not open to everyone but is reserved exclusively for authorized organizations. Determining the number and identity of the organizations authorized to participate is, therefore, the first step in designing a network. For its part, each organization constitutes a specific trust domain that governs its own set of peers and manages its digital identities through a specific MSP.

Similarly, transactions carried out between members belonging to a specific trust domain must be validated by referring to specific endorsement policies. From what has been said, it is clear that it is necessary to define in advance and in detail each trust domain to which an organization belongs, establishing the endorsement policies and the MSP and ordering services that characterize it, before deploying Hyperledger Fabric. Managing an instance of Hyperledger Fabric is an expensive operation that requires both skills and an adequate budget from the organization.

Organizations that decide to implement their permissioned blockchain using Hyperledger Fabric are called to carry out a series of assessments on the overall governance of the network.

Hyperledger Fabric network governance

Some of the decisions to be made by organizations regarding governance are to do with the following:

- How to verify members at first network startup
- How to manage the process of joining new members following the startup of the network
- Which counterparties are authorized to deploy chaincodes within the network
- How transaction information should be stored in the blockchain to meet the confidentiality needs of the counterparties

Decisions need to be made as to who will manage the ordering service and how many different ordering services will be admissible within the network. Usually, the ordering service is combined with the MSP, but keep in mind that in Hyperledger Fabric, the ordering service takes on a central importance in terms of the security and confidentiality of transactions. The ordering service is in fact able to inspect all the transactions, and the information contained in them, that it takes charge of. Organizations may, therefore, decide to entrust an independent third party with the ordering service, or they may decide to reserve this task for trusted entities. These aspects must obviously be decided and agreed between the organizations participating in the network before implementing Hyperledger Fabric.

In the next section, we will learn more about Hyperledger's membership provider.

MSP

Once the network governance policies have been established, we are able to associate the respective digital identities to individual entities. The MSP is the component of Hyperledger Fabric that's responsible for the creation and management of these digital identities. The default MSP implementation offered by Hyperledger Fabric is Fabric CA. Fabric CA allows the registration of users belonging to a member organization of the network, associating them with digital identities in the form of X.509 certificates. It is the responsibility of the participating organizations to establish, during the permissioned blockchain design phase, the policies envisaged for the admission of new members. The default policy states that the admission of new members is decided with the absolute majority of the candidates, but organizations can establish a different criterion.

In the following section, we will learn more about Fabric CA configuration.

Fabric CA configuration

There are two configuration methods for Fabric CA:

- Standalone mode
- The LDAP server

To start the service in standalone mode, you need to assign a digital identity to be stored in the backend database, which by default is an instance of SQLite. To interact with the Fabric CA service in standalone mode, the administrator must perform an identity enroll, which consists of sending a **certificate signing request** (**CSR**) to Fabric CA and obtaining an X.509 certificate as a response.

Once the X.509 certificate is obtained, the administrator is able to add other users to Fabric CA.

The operations provided by Fabric CA are as follows:

- Registering new members
- Enrolling members
- Revoking digital identities

Let's look at the relevant aspects of these operations.

Registration operation

By registering, a new member identifier is added within Fabric CA. Be careful that the register operation does not issue the X.509 certificate associated with the new member; to do this, it is necessary to proceed with the enrolling operation. The identifier used to register the new member can be freely chosen by the Fabric CA administrator, or determined by the policies defined when designing the network. Once this identification ID has been established (for example, the user's email), it will be encoded within the certificate returned in the enrollment phase.

Since Hyperledger Fabric version 1.1, during the registration phase, it is possible to associate to members some attributes, which will be encoded in the X.509 certificate in the next enrollment phase. As an example of an attribute that can be assigned to the user during registration, it could be the role covered within the organization. These attributes could be used to limit some operations to certain categories of user, during the execution of chaincodes. The subsequent update of the attributes assigned during the registration phase is, however, a very impractical operation, as it requires the revocation of the certificate containing the attributes to be updated. Following registration, if Fabric CA is started in standalone mode, the service will create a user password if it has not been defined during registration. This password will be used to make the enrollment request by the newly registered user.

Enrollment operation

Users with identifiers and passwords can enroll in the Fabric CA service. Enrollment consists of forwarding the CSR, following which Fabric CA will issue X.509 certificates associated with the user. Attention must be paid to the number of enrollment requests that the individual user is authorized to submit, because in response to each new enrollment request, Fabric CA will issue a new X.509 certificate.

Fabric CA must be configured in such a way as to prevent an unlimited number of enrollment requests from the same user, limiting the requests to a predetermined number. Allowing users to submit multiple enrollment requests can make sense in some contexts and for specific use cases, but it makes managing identity revocation complex.

Revoking digital identities

To revoke a digital identity within Hyperledger Fabric, it is necessary to issue the standard **certificate revocation lists** (**CRLs**). The CRLs must be forwarded to all the organizations belonging to the network, to ensure that the revoked identities and their certificates are promptly detected by all the peers of the network.

Now let's move on to another aspect that characterizes Hyperledger Fabric: the ability to execute smart contracts in compliance with security policies.

Hyperledger chaincode security

Smart contracts, which in Hyperledger Fabric take the name of chaincodes, are programs containing instructions regarding transactions and are characterized by self-execution, meaning that when a trigger event occurs, the instructions contained in the smart contract are executed. In Hyperledger Fabric, chaincodes can be programmed using standard programming languages.

 Please note that chaincodes do not have direct access to the transaction ledger, and only after their execution will the transactions be added to the ledger.

Chaincodes can be deployed by peer nodes, even in multiple versions of the same program.

In the next section, we'll see how the installation and deployment of chaincodes is carried out.

Installing and deploying chaincodes

Since the installation of chaincodes is a delicate operation, it requires elevated privileges in order to be performed. In order to install a chaincode on a peer node, the entity performing the installation must possess a certificate, recognized by the MSP, to be installed on the node. A chaincode can refer to a specific endorsement policy, requesting a digital signature as an endorsement by a peer; the chaincode must, therefore, be installed on all the endorsing peers.

Once the chaincode is installed, the members of a channel can deploy and instantiate the chaincode on the channel, based on the deployment policies that have previously been agreed between the members. The chaincodes can also be shared with other endorsing peers that belong to organizations that are taking part in the network managed with Hyperledger Fabric.

In the following section, we'll learn more about chaincode security.

Chaincode security

Since chaincodes can also be developed by unreliable third parties and contain instructions written in general-purpose programming languages, in order to guarantee the security of the architecture, they are executed in separate Docker containers. The different versions of the chaincodes are also executed in separate containers.

However, these Docker containers still have access to the virtual network, in addition to the network in general; any misconfigurations of the node where the chaincode is installed can, therefore, affect the virtual network, too. Since the chaincode must be installed on all endorsing peers, to ensure the integrity of the chaincode in the sharing phase with the other peers, it is possible to resort to the encryption of chaincodes.

Since chaincodes must be installed on all endorsing peers, it is necessary to ensure the integrity of the chaincodes through cryptographic mechanisms while sharing them with other peers.

In the next section, we'll take care of chaincode trusted execution.

Chaincode trusted execution

One of the problems with smart contracts is preserving confidentiality. Since the data of the smart contracts is replicated on all the nodes of a network, how can the confidentiality of the transactions be guaranteed? One of the proposed solutions consists of combining a **trusted execution environment** (**TEE**) with the blockchain. Introducing TEEs prevents the possibility that untrusted network nodes can access the data contained within the TEE. However, not all types of blockchains are suitable for the introduction of a TEE.

In particular, blockchains that use PoW consensus mechanisms do not finalize the status of transactions. Therefore, the execution of a smart contract must necessarily manage rollbacks, which should instead be avoided to ensure the confidentiality of the data. One of the proposed solutions is the implementation of TEEs at the hardware level, as in the case of Intel's **Software Guard Extensions** (**SGX**). SGX represents one of the most promising technological solutions—it defines trusted execution contexts at the CPU level (CPU enclaves), consequently isolating both programs and data at the hardware level.

In the next section, we will learn more about trusted execution with Intel SGX.

Trusted execution with Intel SGX

SGX allows platforms such as Hyperledger Fabric to run chaincodes in trusted execution contexts (CPU enclaves). In essence, a CPU enclave isolates a memory area by exploiting hardware control mechanisms. In so doing, the CPU enclave guarantees the integrity and confidentiality of the enclave even in the event of a compromise of the host operating system.

Furthermore, an enclave is able to demonstrate to another entity (such as a peer or a client) whether a specific chaincode is already running, through a procedure known as remote attestation. The memory areas protected by the CPU enclaves are, however, volatile, and their status gets lost without the possibility of recovery in the case of the restarting or crashing of the enclave.

To this end, SGX supports data sealing, through which it is possible to persist the state of the enclave on storage, after having encrypted the data and the execution status of the enclave. Data sealing, while guaranteeing the confidentiality of the data, does not, however, prevent the possibility of rollback attacks.

Now let's have a look at the most common security threats affecting Hyperledger Fabric.

Preventing common threats with Hyperledger

Hyperledger Fabric manages some of the most common threats by leveraging its own architectural security model. Obviously, this does not exempt those who administer the platform from adopting the appropriate perimeter measures (firewall, routing, and so on) to safeguard the security of network infrastructures.

Common security threats can relate to the following:

- **The identity of the participants**: A typical attack consists of using stolen user credentials to authenticate on the system as an authorized user. The management of the X.509 digital certificates, made possible by Fabric CA, limits this type of attack, provided that the CRL is constantly updated and shared with all the member organizations.
- **Data integrity and confidentiality**: Hyperledger Fabric's transaction management mechanisms, combined with the use of cryptography, is an effective means of preventing threats to data integrity and confidentiality.

- **The availability of the service**: To prevent DoS attacks, traditional security measures must be adopted (network perimeters, firewalls, routing, and so on).
- **Endpoint viruses and malware**: Here, security measures should be taken regardless of the features offered by Hyperledger Fabric.

There are also some specific threats that target the individual components of Hyperledger Fabric and require the correct configuration of Hyperledger as well as the correct management of network infrastructures as prevention measures.

In the next section, we will delve deeper into the Hyperledger Fabric ecosystem.

The Hyperledger Fabric ecosystem

One of the most delicate security aspects of Hyperledger Fabric is the heterogeneity of the components that make up the platform. In fact, Hyperledger needs several auxiliary tools to manage the functions. For example, the implementation of the ordering service, one of the central components of the architecture, is usually carried out using Apache Kafka and ZooKeeper, which are necessary for the management of messaging and service discovery.

Other components, such as Apache CouchDB, can be used to track recent transactions added to the ledger. This heterogeneity of the components determines evident difficulties in the management of Hyperledger security, as it requires specific skills for each individual component. Just think, for example, of the number of communication ports that must be monitored in order to ensure the functioning of the platform.

A typical Hyperledger installation, which also includes Kafka and ZooKeeper, requires that the communication ports of the corresponding network services are accessible:

- Ordering service: **7050**
- ZooKeeper (ordering service): **2181, 2888, 3888**
- Kafka (ordering service): **9000, 9092**
- Fabric CA: **7054**
- Peers: **7051, 7053, 8053**
- Docker: **2377, 7946, 4789**

Even this simple list helps us to understand that we have to pay the necessary attention to limiting access to these network services, preventing possible unauthorized connections from outside the network perimeter.

Peer nodes, on the other hand, must be able to connect to each other to form a peer-to-peer network. Likewise, client nodes must be able to directly reach peers, the Fabric CA service, and the ordering service. Managing the firewall rules carefully may not, therefore, be an easy operation, due to the complexity of the network.

In the following section, we will see how to run Hyperledger on Docker.

Running Hyperledger on Docker

Not surprisingly, many administrators decide to install the entire Hyperledger Fabric architecture on Docker. Here also, however, there are still problems, and care must be taken to ensure that the processes in the containers are not run with root privileges, just as the containers are not started with root privileges. At the same time, it is necessary to verify who can have access to the Docker system group, since they can manage the containers deployed on the host.

The next section explains Hyperledger transaction privacy.

Hyperledger transaction privacy

Hyperledger Fabric offers a number of mechanisms aimed at preserving transaction privacy. Let's see the main ones in the following sections.

Channels

The availability of multi-channel functionality allows segregating information that belongs to different channels. In this way, only peers participating in the same channel are able to archive transaction data. Peers belonging to the same channel, in fact, share the same ledger. Hyperledger Fabric allows you to combine multiple blockchains with the same ordering service, and each separate blockchain is identified as a separate channel, along with its member nodes. Although separated into different channels, transaction data is still visible from the ordering service.

Private data

It is possible to establish which peers of a given channel can see transaction data, while the remaining peers and the ordering service have access only to the hash digests of the transaction data. In this way, transaction data is made private (private data) and shared only between authorized peers. Therefore, only the hashes calculated on transaction data are forwarded to the remaining peers and to the ordering service. Within the blockchain, no private data will be stored, but only hashes calculated on private data.

Summary

In this chapter, we have seen the differences between permissionless (public) and permissioned (private) blockchains and the main implications of different consensus mechanisms and transaction management. We also addressed the various architectural, application-related, and security-related aspects of Hyperledger Fabric, one of the most popular enterprise-class permissioned blockchains, highlighting the advantages of adopting a modular architecture with Hyperledger Fabric. Special attention was paid to trusted execution environments and preserving transaction privacy by exploiting multi-channel functionality and private data.

In the next chapter, our journey continues with an analysis of the security of decentralized apps and smart contracts in the Ethereum environment.

3
Section 3: Securing Decentralized Apps and Smart Contracts

In this section, you will be introduced to decentralized applications and smart contracts in terms of their design and deployment on the Ethereum platform. After that, you will learn about their security best practices.

This section comprises the following chapters:

- Chapter 6, *Decentralized Apps and Smart Contracts*
- Chapter 7, *Preventing Threats for DApps and Smart Contracts*

6

Decentralized Apps and Smart Contracts

This chapter focuses on the security aspects of **Decentralized Applications (DApps)**. It shows the best practices to be adopted when developing, creating, and executing certain DApps such as smart contracts. The reference platform for our analysis will be the Ethereum environment, as it represents the most widespread platform for the development of DApps. However, most of the concepts that will be described are easily extensible to other development platforms.

The topics covered in the chapter are as follows:

- Introducing DApps
- Introducing smart contract fundamentals
- Creating secure smart contracts
- Executing secure smart contracts

Let's start by analyzing what a DApp is.

Technical requirements

The code files of this chapter can be found on GitHub:
`https://github.com/PacktPublishing/-Securing-Blockchain-Networks-like-Ethereum-and-Hyperledger-Fabric/tree/master/Chapter06`

Check out the following video to see the Code in Action: `https://bit.ly/2VbhqMK`

Introducing DApps

Much of the attractiveness represented by blockchain technology is linked to the possibility of implementing safe and transparent solutions to solve common problems. We can develop DApps to exploit the characteristics of transparency and security made available by the blockchain. This development strategy is thus considered consistent with the logic of decentralization that it is possible to implement with blockchain technology.

In traditional software solutions, data is stored within a centralized server, and access to data is allowed through predefined application interfaces. As such, the architecture of traditional software solutions constitutes a single point of failure.

With the blockchain, however, the data is distributed in a myriad of nodes, in a redundant form, thus preventing the possibility of loss and corruption of the information stored. On the other hand, the blockchain guarantees the transparency of the information, as it is digitally signed and securely referable to the identified counterparties of the transactions.

To take advantage of these specific features offered by the blockchain, it is useful to develop DApps.

In the next section, we look at the different types of DApps.

Types of DApps

Blockchain technology allows us to develop different types of DApps according to our specific needs and use cases.

In the following sections, we'll see the main types of DApps and their characteristics.

Smart contracts

The most common form of DApp is the smart contract. A smart contract is a piece of decentralized software that implements a particular contract, the execution of which is subject to the occurrence of specific events. The blockchain represents the preferred environment of smart contracts, as it guarantees transparency in verifying the fulfillment of the conditions required for their execution.

In fact, smart contracts are automatically executed in the blockchain when the conditions that establish their enforcement are met. Smart contracts can encapsulate the business logic of different use cases, which can range from common legal contracts to the management of financial exchanges and insurance contracts, up to e-government functions.

One of the purposes of smart contracts is to standardize the business logic of the different use cases, thus constituting the basis for the development of other DApps, such as **Decentralized Organizations (DO)** and **Decentralized Autonomous Organizations (DAO)**, which we will examine in the following sections.

Decentralized organizations

The level of abstraction achievable through the blockchain allows us to implement the structure of an entire organization as a DApp.

A DO is the smart contract representation of an organization's structure, with its rules and organizational schema.

The interaction between the constituent parts of the organization, therefore, takes place through the code of the smart contracts that get deployed on the blockchain.

Decentralized autonomous organizations

DAOs are basically similar to DOs, in the sense that DAOs also encapsulate the business logic, organizational rules, and structure of DOs within them.

The difference lies in the autonomous adjective that distinguishes DAOs from DOs: *autonomous* means that DAOs are completely automated and their business logic is managed by algorithms, instead of depending on human intervention.

At present, a DAO is not recognized as a full and shared legal entity, as the standardization of the enforcement rules contained therein must comply with the different laws and jurisdictions in which it can take effect.

After having introduced the main DApp types, in the following sections, we'll look at the characteristics of DApps.

Characteristics of DApps

One of the fundamental characteristics that distinguish DApps from traditional applications is represented by the fact that DApps are developed to be executed on top of the blockchain technology. As such, DApps can benefit from the advantages associated with the blockchain in terms of transparency and security of transactions.

To this end, the development of DApps must respect some fundamental criteria:

- The data relating to the operations carried out through the DApps must be protected by encryption and stored within the blockchain on which they are performed, to prevent any compromise or loss of data.
- The reward due to the blockchain nodes that contribute to increasing the value associated with DApps must be represented by cryptographic tokens.
- Tokens constitute proof of value and must be generated using standard cryptographic algorithms.
- It must be ensured that no node or entity can control the majority of tokens.
- The DApps code should be released as open source.
- Any changes to the applications must be subject to the consent of the community.

The consensus mechanisms adopted by DApps can be both **Proof of Work** (**PoW**) and the **Proof of Stake** (**PoS**). Unlike PoW, PoS recognizes greater power to validate transactions at the node that proves to hold more tokens. Recall that compared to PoW, PoS is more efficient in managing energy resources, and is able to reach consensus more quickly. However, so far, only PoW has proven to be able to resist 51% attacks. The development of DApps is characterized by some particular aspects not common in traditional applications. While, in traditional applications, we are mostly dealing with classes and objects, in the case of DApps, we have to manage elements such as transactions and tokens in addition to addresses, wallets, accounts, and balances. These concepts are typically only found in blockchains.

In the design of a DApp, the first step is usually represented by the representation of the application data within the blockchain. Unlike traditional applications, all data stored within the blockchain is digitally signed by the counterparties participating in the transactions by apposing their private keys. Since private keys are associated with specific public identifiers (addresses), in the development of applications for the blockchain, we must define who can sign certain data. We also need to decide how to represent the behavior of the application in terms of data structures compatible with the blockchain.

After having examined the peculiar characteristics of DApps, in the following section, we introduce Ethereum, which represents one of the most popular development platforms for DApps.

Introducing Ethereum

Developed by Vitalik Buterin, Ethereum was one of the first public blockchains to allow the development and execution of DApps. In Ethereum, DApps are implemented through the development of smart contracts. Smart contracts can be developed using various programming languages, but the most-used programming language is Solidity. Ethereum also provides a digital currency, ether, usable both by accounts and by DApps.

The use of ether is required both for publication and for invoking the methods exposed by a smart contract. Like the Bitcoin public blockchain, there are also two main types of nodes in Ethereum, miner nodes and regular nodes. The functions performed by the different nodes within Ethereum are similar to those of the nodes in Bitcoin: regular nodes forward transactions within the network, while miner nodes validate transactions by mining new blocks. Each node keeps an updated copy of the blockchain.

To join the Ethereum blockchain, it is necessary to create an account, as shown in the following section.

Creating Ethereum accounts

Ethereum accounts are mostly created with Ethereum wallets (more on this at `https://ethereum.org/wallets/`).

To understand what hides under the hood, we will now analyze the account creation process from a cryptographical perspective.

An Ethereum account is made up of an asymmetric pair of cryptographic keys, created through the use of elliptical encryption algorithms. The elliptical encryption algorithm used by Ethereum is based on secp256k1 and makes use of 256-bit encryption. Once the key pair is generated, the public address representative of the Ethereum account must be also generated.

The address associated with the Ethereum account is generated from the public key using the following procedure:

1. Calculate the hash digest of the public key using the keccak-256 hashing algorithm, which returns a numeric value of 256 bits (32 bytes).
2. From the hash digest thus calculated, the first 12 bytes must be eliminated.
3. Encode the remaining 20 bytes of the hash digest in hexadecimal form, thus obtaining the requested address.

Once the address is obtained, it can be used to receive ether.

The transfer of ether from one account to another takes place through transactions, as shown in the following section.

Ethereum transactions

Through transactions, it is possible to transfer ether from one account to another, or from one account to a smart contract, and from a contract to an address. Transactions are also used to invoke the methods exposed by smart contracts, or to deploy them.

The elements making up a transaction are the following:

- The transaction recipient's address
- The sender's signature
- The transaction intention, meaning the smart contract method to be invoked, or the contract deployment request
- The transferred amount of ether
- The gas limit, representing the maximum computational cycles the transaction can execute
- The gas price, representing the cost for the sender associated with each computational cycle

The transfer of a certain amount of ether to an address, or the invocation of a method of a smart contract, is therefore carried out by forwarding the transaction to the network. Before being sent to the network, the transaction must be digitally signed using the sender's private key. A transaction can be considered valid after at least 15 confirmations received from the network nodes.

The network consensus mechanism is used for transaction validation, as shown in the following section.

Ethereum consensus mechanism

As we mentioned in the previous section, *Ethereum transactions*, a transaction must be signed with the sender's private key. Likewise, to be validated, there must be sufficient funds in the account of the sender that instanced the transaction. Following the preliminary validations, the transaction is forwarded to the miner nodes. Once the validity of the transaction has been verified, the miner nodes will insert it into a block, completing the validation of the transaction by mining the block into which it was inserted.

As a result of the mining activity, the block will be forwarded to the nodes of the network. At this point, the nodes in the network are able to verify the transaction using the predefined consensus mechanism. In the case of Ethereum, the consensus mechanism used is PoW, as for Bitcoin. The consensus mechanism prevents transaction data stored in the blockchain from being modified by network nodes. It also allows the nodes to verify, in the presence of different versions of blockchain, which version is the correct one.

In the next section, we'll see how the transactions contained in smart contracts are performed within the Ethereum platform.

The Ethereum Virtual Machine

Smart contracts are executed within a virtual machine, the **Ethereum Virtual Machine (EVM)**. All nodes in the network are able to perform the transactions contained in the smart contracts by launching them in the EVM. The final outcome of the smart contract execution is stored by the nodes in the network storage.

To avoid the rapid saturation of computational resources and network storage, a transaction cost, expressed in terms of *gas*, is associated with each execution, as we'll see in the next section.

Ethereum gas

Gas represents the unit of measurement for the transaction costs associated with the execution of the transactions. Therefore, each transaction has a limit, expressed in units of gas, up to which it is willing to spend to execute the transaction. As such, the transaction is carried out only if the computational costs are lower than or equal to the gas limit. Within EVM, in fact, each operation is associated with a cost expressed in units of gas.

In the following section, we see how shared resources are managed within Ethereum.

Ethereum communication and storage protocols

Ethereum uses two special protocols for communication management and storage management within the network. These protocols are **Whisper** for decentralized communication, and **Swarm** for decentralized storage. The Whisper protocol allows network nodes to communicate with each other, both directly and by sending broadcast messages. DApps can also use Whisper to establish secure communication channels between them (as in the case of a chat), using the SSH protocol.

Network storage is managed through the Swarm protocol, which represents a decentralized filesystem. Within the decentralized filesystem, both data and DApps' code can be stored, as well as blockchain data. Swarm was designed as a peer-to-peer storage protocol, with the characteristics of being fault-tolerant and resistant to denial-of-service attacks.

In the next section, we'll see Ethereum's main security threats.

Ethereum security threats

The main security threats that afflict Ethereum are as follows:

- Stale blocks
- Blockchain forks
- Catastrophic bugs

We will go into the details of each security threat in the following sections.

Stale blocks

The problem of stale blocks (*uncle blocks* in Ethereum parlance) occurs where two or more miner nodes mine the next block to be inserted in the blockchain at almost the same time. In similar cases, the blockchain cannot store two valid blocks with the same block number, and must, therefore, make a choice on which block to keep, and which block to discard. The valid blocks that are not inserted in the blockchain are thus called stale blocks. Due to the presence of the stale blocks, the miner nodes risk not receiving from the network the reward they deserve. In fact, they may even waste their computational power in mining invalid blocks that get discarded.

Stale blocks are a problem from several points of view. First, the presence of stale blocks delays the confirmation of valid transactions, which, to be confirmed, must therefore wait for multiple nodes before being successfully validated. In addition, stale blocks also pose a problem for blockchain security and integrity. Due to the presence of multiple blocks mined at almost the same time, which compete with each other to assume the role of the next block to be appended to the blockchain, the blockchain may run into the phenomenon known as forking, as we know from `Chapter 3`, *Blockchain Security Assumptions*.

Blockchain forking means that we end up with two different versions of the blockchain. To verify which blockchain version is the correct one, we use the consensus mechanism, which, in the case of Ethereum (as in Bitcoin), is the PoW protocol. PoW allows the nodes to determine the correct version of the blockchain, based on the greater difficulty associated with each conflicting version of the blockchain. The blockchain characterized by greater complexity will therefore constitute the final version of the blockchain accepted by the network.

One way to prevent the problem of stale blocks is therefore to increase the average block generation time. This would result in increasing the difficulty of the math challenge that the miner nodes must solve, in order to mine the new blocks. The presence of the stale blocks therefore decreases proportionally to the increase in the average time required for the mining of the new blocks. In addition, the increase in difficulty contributes to making the blockchain more secure against attempts to alter transaction data. The disadvantage associated with the increase in average mining time is the reduced number of validated transactions per unit of time.

Ethereum therefore manages the problem of stale blocks using the GHOST protocol. **GHOST** stands for **Greedy Heaviest Observed Subtree**, and was introduced in 2013 on the Ethereum platform to prevent the rising of stale blocks by increasing mining difficulty. To increase the difficulty of the blockchain, the GHOST protocol encourages miners to insert stale blocks into the blockhain. The overall difficulty of the blockchain will therefore be increased. By including the stale blocks along with the valid blocks, we may incur a conflict between the transactions contained in the valid blocks and in the stale blocks. To prevent any conflicts, the transactions contained in the stale blocks are not considered in the calculation of the confirmations necessary to validate transactions.

Additionally, the miner nodes that mined the stale blocks will still receive a reward, but this will be less than the reward awarded to the nodes that mined valid blocks. Finally, the GHOST protocol limits the number of stale blocks that each block (called **nephews**, to be consistent with **uncle blocks**) can refer to, thus preventing miner nodes from engaging in the exclusive mining of stale blocks.

We said that one of the possible consequences of stale blocks is the blockchain forking phenomenon; however, forking can also occur for other reasons, as we will see in the next section.

Blockchain forks

In the presence of conflicts within the blockchain, different types of forks can occur:

- Temporary forks
- Soft forks
- Hard forks

Temporary forks occur in the presence of multiple blocks that are mined almost at the same time, as in the case of stale blocks. Anyway, the resulting bifurcation of the blockchain is considered temporary, as the decision on the correct version of the blockchain is made by the network choosing the blockchain with greater complexity, based on the PoW consensus mechanism. The soft and hard forks are instead determined by changes in the source code, which can cause conflicts within the blockchain.

Given the frequent changes that have so far affected the Ethereum source code, the platform has faced several cases of both soft and hard forks. The difference between soft and hard forks is determined by the amount of network hash power needed to resolve the conflict between different versions of the blockchain. In the event that the version update is required only for the miner nodes that hold more than 50% of the hash rate, we are in the presence of a soft fork. Where it is necessary that all the nodes of the network upgrade to the new version, we are in the presence of a hard fork.

In addition to stale blocks and forks, blockchain integrity problems can also be determined by the presence of bugs within DApps, as we will see in the following section.

Catastrophic bugs – the DAO bug

The presence of bugs within DApps can cause catastrophic effects, as in the case of the famous DAO bug. As we saw in the *Types of DApps* section of this chapter, a DAO is a special DApp whose code is representative of an organization and its business model. One of the first DAOs was the DAO project, launched in April 2016, with the aim of creating a venture capital fund entirely represented by a decentralized entity, without a central entity in the role of the owner.

DAO was funded through crowdfunding, and has been implemented in the form of smart contracts. Due to the presence of some bugs within the source code of smart contracts, DAO suffered a hacker attack in June 2016, which resulted in the unauthorized transfer of $50 million to the attackers' accounts. To reverse the unauthorized transaction, and recover illicitly withdrawn funds, it was necessary to resort to a hard fork of the Ethereum blockchain.

The possible presence of bugs within smart contracts has therefore raised a controversy in the developer community, regarding the methods of development and debugging intended to ensure the security and quality of the DApps code. On many sides, it was even considered inappropriate to resort to Turing-complete programming languages for the development of smart contracts. This is due to the risks they pose to the integrity of the blockchain (we will deal with Turing-complete languages later on in this chapter).

The use of the hard fork, however necessary it was to recover the funds and cancel the illegal transactions, was nonetheless deemed not in accordance with the logic that inspired the decentralized development model promoted by blockchain technology. The contrasts on the hard fork gave rise to the Ethereum Classic blockchain, which retained the original version of the blockchain before the hard fork took place.

To fully understand the security implications related to the development of smart contracts, in the next section, we will analyze more closely the characteristics of these particular DApps.

Introducing smart contract fundamentals

Smart contracts were first theorized by Nick Szabo, defining them in a 1994 article (available at `http://firstmonday.org/ojs/index.php/fm/article/view/548`) as an electronic transaction protocol designed to execute the terms and conditions of a contract without depending on trusted intermediaries due to the minimization of execution exceptions.

These objectives are achieved by automating the contractual clauses embedded into the software and made self-enforcing by resorting to automated settlements, without the need for legal systems or trusted intermediaries.

Originally, smart contracts were implemented in limited form in Bitcoin, through the use of scripts developed in a non-Turing-complete language. Scripts allowed the transfer of Bitcoins between users of the network without the need to resort to reliable intermediaries.

In the next section, we'll examine the minimal smart contract requirements.

Smart contract requirements

The typical characteristics of a smart contract are the following:

- Self-execution
- Self-enforcing
- Being secure and unstoppable
- Being comprehensible by both humans and computers

Of the previous features, the only ones that are really mandatory are just the first two, while the other two are only optional, nice-to-have requirements. Thus, a smart contract is basically a computer program that implements contractual conditions made automatically executable, and enforceable when certain conditions occur.

In the following section, we'll show how smart contracts automate the execution and the enforcement of contractual terms.

Automating execution and enforcement

The adjective *smart* refers to the characteristic of smart contracts to be fully automated, even in the phase of enforcement of the contractual conditions, based on the occurrence of the events requested for their execution. Unlike traditional legal contracts, which need reliable legal institutions and intermediaries to guarantee their compliance (that is, *legal enforcement*), smart contracts rely exclusively on their self-enforcement capability, in compliance with the **Code-is-Law** clause.

Szabo's pioneering contribution in theorizing smart contracts lies precisely in having foreseen the ability of these automated contracts to be both self-executable and self-enforcing. The specific feature of self-enforcement therefore lies in the ability of smart contracts to automatically enforce all contractual terms. This enforcement is achieved even in spite of adverse events or the behavior of the counterparties, both of which could affect their effective realization.

If the self-execution and self-enforcement properties are considered indispensable for the implementation of smart contracts, the remaining secure and unstoppable properties, although optional, are nonetheless highly in demand, as we will see in the next section.

Secure and unstoppable

One of the growing needs is that smart contracts execute their instructions safely, without being altered by external events, thus guaranteeing the integrity of the contractual terms. Moreover, smart contracts should not be subject to possible interruptions, which can prevent enforcement of the contract.

In other words, smart contracts must guarantee that they will execute the exact instructions provided by the contract on the occurrence of the event that realizes the conditions. As a consequence, the results will not be altered or differ from those expected, thereby preventing the possibility of interruption. To achieve these requirements (being secure and unstoppable) smart contracts must be designed and developed in order to guarantee fault tolerance and the predictability of the final results.

In particular, the predictability of the final results allows smart contracts to be understandable by humans as well as by machines, as we will see in the next section.

Bridging the gap between computers and people

The predictability of the final results means that the execution of smart contracts is deterministic, that is to say, we get the same result every time we run them. The requirement of final-result predictability is also prescribed by the very nature of the blockchain, which was designed to validate transactions using a shared consensus mechanism.

The consensus mechanism presupposes the repeatability and verification of the integrity of the transactions by the individual nodes of the network. In compliance with the Code-is-Law principle, the executable code contained in the smart contracts is itself representative of the contractual conditions.

Therefore, it is highly desirable that this code is written in a language that can also be easily understood by human operators, as well as by machines. As such, the contractual conditions established in the contract can be agreed by the counterparts, without the need for intervention on the part of specialized intermediaries.

To build a bridge between smart contracts and people, it is also desirable that input data could be passed to smart contracts.

This is the task performed by Oracles, the topic of the following section.

Feeding data to smart contracts through Oracles

One of the main limitations of smart contracts is their inability to access external data. The ability to access data available from external sources is necessary in certain use cases, for example, in the case in which the smart contract must verify the price reached by an asset to determine the quantity to be purchased of that asset.

One way to provide external data to a smart contract is to use Oracles. Oracles are trusted interfaces that allow the safe transfer of data from external sources to smart contracts. The external sources of data that Oracles can provide range from news and stock prices to data produced by hardware sensors or **Internet of Things** (**IoT**) appliances.

The Oracles are also able to guarantee the reliability of the external data sources, as well as the absence of any manipulation of the transferred data, even by the Oracles themselves. The mechanism for transferring data is usually achieved by letting smart contracts subscribe to the service offered by the Oracles.

In the following section, we will deal with deploying smart contracts on a blockchain.

Deploying smart contracts on a blockchain

In theory, based on Szabo's indications, smart contracts can also be executed outside of a blockchain. In practice, however, the blockchain constitutes the preferred technology on which to deploy decentralized software such as smart contracts. This is due to the decentralized and distributed nature that characterizes the blockchain.

As we said at the beginning of the chapter, one of the most widely used platforms for the development of smart contracts is Ethereum, as it offers native support for both the development and deployment of smart contracts.

The most widely used language for the development of smart contracts in Ethereum is Solidity, which was designed specifically for the development of these special DApps, but it is also possible to use other programming languages, such as JavaScript and Python.

In the following sections, we will show which criteria to adopt when developing secure smart contracts.

Creating secure smart contracts

To create smart contracts on the Ethereum platform, it is necessary to write the code in one of the supported languages (Solidity is the default language), then compile the code, thus obtaining the bytecode for the EVM, and finally deploy the contract on the platform. Unlike other blockchains (such as Bitcoin's), Ethereum supports the development of smart contracts through Turing-complete programming languages.

In the following section, we'll see the consequences of using Turing-complete development languages for smart contract security.

Developing smart contracts with Turing-complete languages

Ethereum was the first smart contract development platform to allow the use of Turing-complete programming languages. A Turing-complete programming language permits any computational instruction to be performed in a program, using particular iterative instructions, loops, and branches, such as conditional instructions. In this way, the programs developed with Turing-compete languages are able to execute any algorithm, in accordance with the theory of universal computational machines, introduced precisely by Alan Turing.

Solidity, Ethereum's default programming language, being a Turing-complete language, allows the development of smart contracts capable of executing any computational algorithm. This is an advantage on the side of flexibility in the business logic of smart contracts, as it becomes possible to implement contracts of arbitrary complexity, but, on the other hand, it represents a serious problem with regard to the security of smart contracts.

The deterministic nature of smart contracts, in fact, requires that they are absolutely free from bugs. The need to guarantee the predictability and repeatability of the results obtained by executing smart contracts within the blockchain, however, contrasts with the Turing-complete nature of the programming languages used to develop them.

To fully understand the security risks associated with the adoption of a Turing-complete programming language in the development of smart contracts, in the next section, we will compare the advantages, as well as the limitations, deriving from the use of a non-Turing-complete language, such as the Bitcoin Script language.

Bitcoin Script

In Bitcoin, it is possible to develop programs similar to smart contracts using the Script language. These programs are called transaction scripts, as they allow the automated transfer of tokens within the blockchain using a series of predefined commands. Unlike Solidity, the Script language provides a limited subset of executable commands. These commands are restricted exclusively to operations strictly necessary for the execution of transactions. Instructions such as iterative cycles, or conditional statements, are not permitted. Therefore, unlike Solidity, the Script language is not a Turing-complete language.

The operations that Script includes are more similar to those of a math calculator, with its predefined and unchangeable functions, rather than a real programming language. Bitcoin's choice to introduce a non Turing-complete language is therefore intentional. It is aimed at preventing possible security threats, such as, for example, denial-of-service attacks, due to the presence of possible bugs in the code that maliciously exploit endless loops.

Furthermore, the impossibility of introducing iterative and conditional instructions into the code guarantees the predictability and repeatability of the results obtained by the execution of the instructions. On the contrary, programs developed with Turing-complete languages suffer from the halting problem typical of Turing machines, as seen in the **Computability** *is not* **decidability** section of Chapter 3, *Blockchain Security Assumptions*. The Script language is also stateless, meaning it does not retain system state information before or after running programs.

This ensures that program execution is immune to possible state changes that may affect the system on which the program is executed, ensuring repeatability of program execution in any environment. The Script language provides a series of predefined commands (called opcodes) that are performed in order from left to right, using a stack-based memory model.

In the following section, we'll see a simple code snippet developed in Script.

Example of Bitcoin Script

Let's imagine we want to calculate the sum of two numerical values, 3 and 7, using the Script language.

The Script instructions are as follows:

```
3 7 OP_ADD 10 OP_EQUAL
```

In the execution phase of the previous instructions, which takes place from left to right, the numerical values 3 and 7 are stored on the stack using the push operation, and on these values the opcode OP_ADD is applied, which calculates the sum of the two numerical values, after being extracted from the stack using the pop operation.

The result of the OP_ADD opcode, equal to 10 (which represents the sum of 3 and 7), is stored on the stack in order to execute the OP_EQUAL opcode, which verifies that the sum obtained is precisely equal to 10, returning in our case the TRUE Boolean value. Although limited, the instructions provided by the Script language are only those strictly necessary for the execution of transactions, thus preventing the possibility of introducing bugs into the code.

The same cannot be said in the case of Turing-complete languages, as we will see in the following section.

Bug inevitability and the risks of Turing-complete programs

The programming experience with Turing-complete languages has demonstrated the practical impossibility of preventing the presence of bugs within source code. Despite the use of specialized tools for checking the quality of the software (code auditing tools), the absence of bugs within the source code is not guaranteed, and these bugs are often discovered by chance, long after the software is released. The presence of bugs is moreover linked to the use of dynamic instructions of Turing-complete languages, such as iterations and conditional instructions, which contribute to an increase in the complexity of the source code. If the level of complexity exceeds the critical threshold, the software begins to show unpredictable behaviors, typical of chaotic systems.

Just like in chaotic systems, even small differences in input data can lead to highly unstable results in output values, making it impossible to predict software behavior with certainty. The inevitable presence of bugs within programs developed with Turing-complete languages can have potentially devastating consequences, in a context of decentralized and distributed execution, such as that of the blockchain. Running buggy software on standalone computers (such as desktop PCs) can cause damage, but this is limited to the specific computer. In addition, the risks associated with these damages, as they are localized to the computer that runs the buggy software, can be reliably predicted and managed accordingly by resorting to insurance contracts.

In the case of the blockchain, however, the decentralized and distributed context that characterizes the execution of smart contracts may affect the entire network. The presence of a bug within a smart contract can therefore affect the entire distributed architecture, being able to mistakenly invoke methods exposed by other smart contracts, with potentially unpredictable cascading effects. The assessment of the risks associated with the presence of bugs within smart contracts consequently becomes extremely difficult due to the imponderability of the negative events associated with them.

It therefore becomes extremely important to prevent the presence of bugs within smart contracts developed with Turing-complete languages such as Solidity, and deployed on blockchain platforms such as Ethereum. In later sections, we will look at the best practices recommended to prevent the presence of bugs in your code.

In the meantime, let's deal with the development tools that can be used for the Ethereum platform, which is the topic of the next section.

Developing smart contracts with Remix IDE

Among the tools for developing smart contracts with Solidity, the best known is definitely Remix. Remix is an **Integrated Development Environment** (**IDE**) executable located directly within the web browser, without the need for installation, that provides a space for the editing of source code and the compilation and deployment of smart contracts:

1. To access Remix IDE, simply open `http://remix.ethereum.org` in your favorite web browser.

In the following screenshot, we can see the Remix IDE home page:

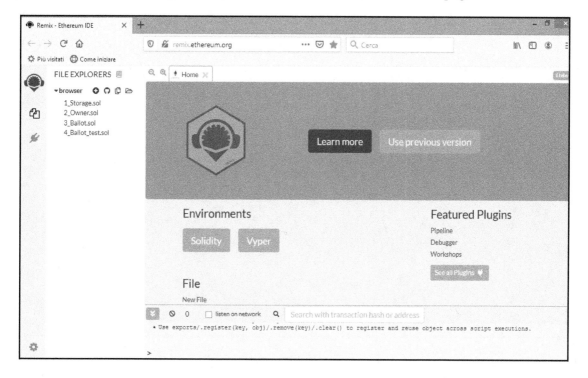

On the Remix home page, there are some default example source codes of smart contracts; it is obviously possible to modify them to our liking, or to add or create our source codes from scratch, using the icons available on the left panel.

In the following screenshot, we see some Solidity code examples:

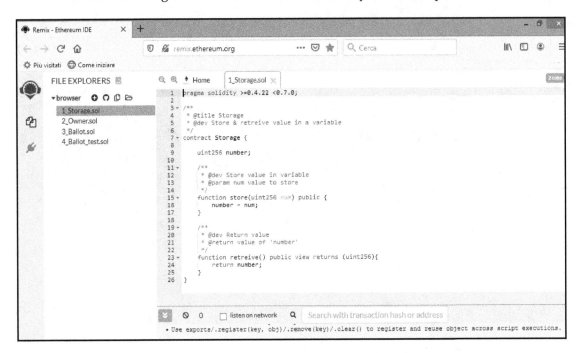

Once the source code has been successfully edited, it is possible to compile it using the Solidity compiler by selecting the Solidity environment on the home page.

The following screenshot shows the Remix Solidity compiler:

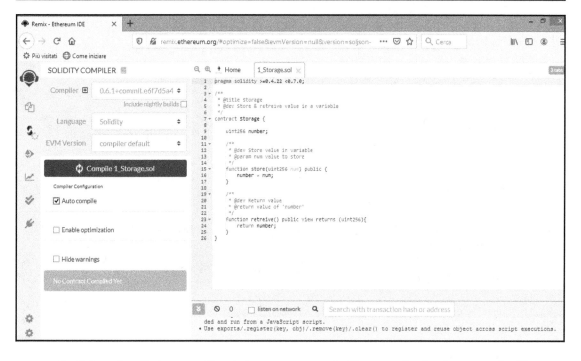

2. Select the **Auto compile** option to automatically compile the source code files as they get updated.
3. Deployment and testing of smart contracts can be performed with the commands on the **Run** tab.

Having introduced the Remix **Graphical User Interface** (**GUI**), in the following section, we will see a simple example of smart contract implementation with Solidity.

A simple smart contract

In the following example, we will develop a simple smart contract in Solidity, which we will call **Greetings**. The first instruction we will insert is the version of `pragma`, which defines the version of the compiler to be used to compile the source code; in our case, the compiler's requested version is 0.4.24:

```
pragma solidity ^0.4.24;
```

To define the contract, we use the `contract` keyword, followed by the name attributed to the smart contract (in our case, `Greetings`) delimited by curly brackets:

```
contract Greetings {
  // smart contract solidity code
}
```

Inside the contract, we add the `printGreetings()` method preceded by the `function` keyword:

```
function printGreetings() public view returns (string) {
    return "Greetings from solidity";
}
```

The `printGreetings()` method returns a string, and is defined as public. Therefore, it is invocable by third parties.

This is the complete source code of our smart contract:

```
pragma solidity ^0.4.24;

contract Greetings {
    function printGreetings() public view returns (string) {
        return "Greetings from solidity";
    }
}
```

We can then compile the source code manually or by selecting the **Auto compile** option in the Remix interface. Once verified that the compiler has not returned any errors or warnings, the contract can be deployed. It should be noted that the methods used in our smart contract are freely usable and do not involve costs in terms of units of gas.

In the next section, we will see how to execute secure smart contracts while respecting smart contract security best practices.

Executing secure smart contracts

As we know, smart contracts in Ethereum are executed within the EVM. The EVM is a virtual machine that also acts as a sandbox, thus preventing smart contracts from directly accessing the network and other shared resources of the blockchain. To update the data stored within the blockchain, the only viable way is therefore to instantiate a transaction, which must be validated by the network nodes. Transactions can also be instantiated by smart contracts.

In the following sections, we will see the best practices that we can adopt to ensure the security of transactions within smart contracts.

Best practices for smart contract security

Smart contracts represent a relatively recent innovation. Therefore, many security problems related to their development are still being analyzed and studied. To prevent the presence of bugs within smart contracts, it is, therefore, useful to follow best practices (as we'll be doing in `Chapter 7`, *Preventing Threats for DApps and Smart Contracts*) that extend and integrate the general principles of software design. One of the principles to follow is to keep the source code simple and modular. The presence of bugs is, in fact, directly proportional to the complexity and length of the source code.

Reducing the size of the code by developing it in a modular form helps to reduce the overall complexity accordingly, also improving the readability and maintainability of the source code. It is equally important to simplify the logic of the program by reducing the number of exceptions that can contribute to increasing the complexity and unpredictability of the results. There are also some specific characteristics of the Ethereum platform that must be kept in mind when developing smart contracts.

First of all, it must be remembered that in Ethereum, every executable instruction involves a cost in terms of gas, and that there is a limit to the number of computational resources that a transaction can use for each individual block. Furthermore, with Ethereum being a public blockchain, everyone can see the information entered within the transactions, and therefore there are no truly private variables. Therefore, DApps should only be used when strictly necessary. To reduce the risk of bugs in the development of smart contracts, it is also advisable to use libraries and function modules that are widely tested.

 One of the most popular libraries that offers the most common features for the development of smart contracts is OpenZeppelin, available at `https://github.com/OpenZeppelin/openzeppelin-solidity/`.

Dealing with bugs in smart contracts

In the event that, despite following all precautions, the presence of bugs should occur, it is important to understand how best to manage these bugs to minimize their negative impact. One of the problems with the management of bugs in smart contracts is the fact that once deployed, smart contracts are unmodifiable. Therefore, it is not possible to fix bugs as we can in traditional applications by simply updating the source code.

In order to minimize the possible negative impact of bugs, it is possible to place limits on the amounts that can be transferred or withdrawn, requiring the use of multi-signature approval to overcome these limits. It is also possible to implement appropriate functions that provide customized features within smart contracts that can suspend or delay their execution in the event of the discovery of bugs.

Summary

In this chapter, we introduced DApps and their characteristics. We explored the fundamentals of smart contracts, with particular reference to the Ethereum platform. We understood the potential risks associated with the presence of software bugs in smart contracts developed with Turing-complete programming languages. We also learned how to create and execute secure smart contracts using the best practices for assuring smart contract security.

In the next chapter, we will deal with threat prevention and analysis of the most common attacks targeting DApps.

7
Preventing Threats for DApps and Smart Contracts

In the previous chapter, *Decentralized Apps and Smart Contracts*, we introduced **Distributed Applications (DApps)** and smart contracts, highlighting the risks associated with using Turing-complete programming languages such as Solidity. In this chapter, we will deal in detail with the threats associated with the most common smart contract vulnerabilities. We will also see which tools can be used to analyze smart contracts, in search of possible vulnerabilities present in the source code. Some tools we'll see are useful in preventing the exploitation of these vulnerabilities by attackers.

The topics we will cover in this chapter are as follows:

- Hacking smart contracts
- Smart contract threats
- Smart contract attack examples
- Preventing smart contract attacks
- Analyzing smart contracts for security

We begin the chapter by analyzing the hacking techniques applied to smart contracts, which is the subject of the following section.

Technical requirements

The code files of this chapter can be found on GitHub:
https://github.com/PacktPublishing/-Securing-Blockchain-Networks-like-Ethereum-and-Hyperledger-Fabric/tree/master/Chapter07

Check out the following video to see the Code in Action: https://bit.ly/2UUlIJl

Hacking smart contracts

The still-experimental nature of smart contracts requires us to give adequate attention to the security aspects of these special DApps. Damage resulting from vulnerabilities present in smart contracts can have a significant impact on the entire architecture of the underlying blockchain. In fact, once deployed on the blockchain, smart contracts cannot be edited. The executable code of smart contracts takes the form of bytecode interpreted by a special **virtual machine** (**VM**), which, in the case of Ethereum, is **Ethereum Virtual Machine** (**EVM**). To check the presence of vulnerabilities within smart contracts, it is possible to perform a code review of the source code, but there are some specific tools that allow even the bytecode produced during the compilation phase to be analyzed.

One of the first tools created for the verification of smart contracts is MAIAN, which we will introduce in the next section.

Introducing MAIAN

MAIAN is one of the first tools for the automatic detection of Ethereum smart contract bugs. MAIAN is developed in Python and is available for download from `https://github.com/MAIAN-tool/MAIAN`. The tool is released under the **Massachusetts Institute of Technology** (**MIT**) License (`https://opensource.org/licenses/MIT`), so it can be freely employed for both private and commercial use. MAIAN is known to successfully run on Linux and macOS.

To run MAIAN, you need to meet the following list of tools and library dependencies:

- Go Ethereum: `https://ethereum.github.io/go-ethereum/install/`
- Solidity compiler: `http://solidity.readthedocs.io/en/develop/installing-solidity.html`
- Z3 Theorem Prover: `https://github.com/Z3Prover/z3`
- The Web3 Python library (which can also be run on Python 3)

Run the following command at the Command Prompt:

```
pip install web3
```

To run MAIAN in a console and get the full list of options, just type the following command at the Command Prompt:

```
python maian.py -h
```

MAIAN also comes in a graphical version.

To run the MAIAN **graphical user interface** (**GUI**), you also need to install the PyQt5 Python library. To launch the GUI-based version of MAIAN , simply run the following command:

```
python gui-maian.py
```

In the next section, we'll learn how to analyze smart contracts with MAIAN.

Analyzing smart contracts with MAIAN

The peculiarity of MAIAN is that it is able to analyze both the source code and the bytecode of smart contracts to build a trace of transactions, to find and confirm bugs.

The bytecode of a smart contract takes the form represented in the following example, which shows an extract of the bytecode of the example_suicidal.bytecode smart contract, available in the example_contracts MAIAN directory:

```
0x60606040523615610082576e060020a6000350463416ce86f81146100
8457806341c0e1b5146101535780634e69d560146101645780635f2ef085
1461017d5780636d4ce63c1461022c578063877d0cd7146103d157806389
3d20e81461049e578063be1c766b146104be578063c8691b2a146104c657
8063e21d9b51146105a5575b005b6100827340563c8a47996ba3e9afd51c
ef23070a9fd35d7533600160a060020a03161480156100bd575060035461
0100900460ff166001145b806100f9575073f9968bbbadf98cd736f77374
68dbbb6c9d3e62d33600160a060020a03161480156100f95750600354610
```

```
...
```

```
602084015260039290930191909152825460016a060020a0319161760a0
60020a67ffffffffffffffff02191660a360020a607d029091021760e060
020a60ff0219167c030000000000000000000000000000000000000000
0000000000000017905550565b505050600092835250602091829020604
8051606081018252333808252426103e881029683019690965260049190920
015291018054600160a060020a03191690911760a060020a67ffffffffff
ffffff02191660a360020a607d029092029190911760e060020a60ff0219
1660e260020a17905556
```

To analyze the bytecode of a smart contract with MAIAN, you can run the following command:

```
python maian.py -b <bytecode file>
```

In the case of smart contracts in source code format, you can run the following command:

```
python maian.py -s <contract file> <main contract name>
```

Another interesting feature of MAIAN is that it uses a private blockchain to deploy contracts, in order to reduce the number of false positives.

Upon launching the tool, therefore, an Ethereum blockchain instance is executed in the background and is terminated, except in exceptional cases, when MAIAN finishes the search for bugs. MAIAN confirms the presence of bugs by sending appropriate transactions to the contracts.

To understand how MAIAN works, in the next section, we will analyze the different types of buggy smart contracts.

Types of buggy smart contracts

As we already know, once deployed on the blockchain, smart contracts are unmodifiable. The discovery of bugs within smart contracts after their deployment thus prevents their code from being updated. If prevention and management measures for the bugs—shown in Chapter 6, *Decentralized Apps and Smart Contracts*—have not been adopted, the only alternative that remains is to perform a suicide instruction within the contract.

Once the contract enters the killed status, it can no longer receive or send transactions. The problem remains that, once a vulnerability identified within smart contracts has been successfully exploited by attackers, illicit transactions already performed can neither be canceled nor reversed without carrying out a blockchain hard fork.

This is why it is of fundamental importance to identify the possible presence of bugs within smart contracts before deploying them.

The types of exploits affecting smart contracts that MAIAN is able to classify are essentially three, highlighted as follows:

- Suicidal contracts
- Prodigal contracts
- Greedy contracts

In the following sections, we will analyze the individual types.

Suicidal contracts

The ability to perform the `kill` operation is expected to reduce the negative impact of any vulnerabilities found within smart contracts. This operation, however, lends itself to possible misuses by the attackers if not properly implemented. Therefore, smart contracts that can be killed arbitrarily by any users are defined as suicidal.

Prodigal contracts

Smart contracts that allow transactions to be sent to arbitrary addresses are defined as prodigal, thus distributing funds to third parties that have no connection with the contract holder. The vulnerability that is exploited is usually due to the presence of function calls within the smart contract that permit funds to be sent to other contracts or addresses. The implementation of such calls may not include adequate security checks to prevent the illegal use of these functions.

Greedy contracts

Finally, smart contracts capable of only receiving, but not sending, funds are defined as greedy because they prevent the release of the funds received. This may be due to the absence within the contract of the necessary instructions for sending the funds, or due to errors in the implementation of these instructions.

In the following section, we will see how to detect the presence of the different types of buggy contracts using MAIAN.

Checking buggy contract types with MAIAN

To check the different types of buggy contracts using MAIAN, you can take advantage of the following tool options:

- Suicidal contracts: `-c 0`
- Prodigal contracts: `-c 1`
- Greedy contracts: `-c 2`

For example, if we wanted to check whether the `WalletLibrary` smart contract defined in the `ParityWalletLibrary.sol` source code is a suicidal contract, we would have to run MAIAN as follows:

```
python maian.py -s ParityWalletLibrary.sol WalletLibrary -c 0
```

Upon executing the preceding command, you should see the following output:

```
[ ] Compiling Solidity contract from the file ParityWalletLibrary.sol
[ ] Connecting to PRIVATE blockchain emptychain  ... ESTABLISHED
[ ] Deploying contract .... confirmed at address:
0x9583ca884c1d93458fb61ed137ff44f6
...
[ ] Check if contract is SUICIDAL
...
[-] Suicidal vulnerabilty found!
[ ] Confirming suicide vulnerability on private chain ... ..... tx[0] mined
....
tx[1] mined ...

Confirmed ! The contract is suicidal !
```

The `ParityWalletLibrary.sol` source code is freely available in the MAIAN `example_contracts` directory.

In the next section, we will analyze in more detail the main vulnerabilities and threats affecting smart contracts.

Analyzing smart contract threats

The main threats affecting smart contracts are usually attributable to weaknesses present within the source code. Over time, a register of such weaknesses, known as the **Smart Contract Weakness Classification** (**SWC**) Registry, has been drawn up, which can be consulted at `https://swcregistry.io/docs/SWC-100`.

The SWC Registry is released under the MIT License and is freely available at `https://github.com/SmartContractSecurity/SWC-registry`.

The main goals of the SWC Registry are as follows:

- Classifying security issues in smart contracts
- Describing security issues in smart contracts adopting a common language
- Helping training and increasing performance for smart contract analysis tools

In the following sections, we will analyze the main weaknesses present within the source code of smart contracts developed using the Solidity programming language.

Integer overflow and underflow

One of the most common smart contract vulnerabilities is integer overflow and underflow. To understand the characteristics of this vulnerability, it must be remembered that each variable defined within a program has a predefined size in terms of bits, which varies according to the type. In the case of numeric values, they can be stored in variables of different sizes: for example, using the `uint8` type, which represents a byte (8 bits) in size. The maximum numeric value that can be stored inside a variable of type `uint8` is equal to the value determined by the expression $2^8 - 1$, which amounts to 255. Therefore, within a variable of type `uint8`, it is possible to store numeric values that fall in the range from 0 to 255.

What happens if we wanted to store a value greater than 255 inside a variable of type `uint8`, such as—for example—the numeric value 256? In this case, we would face an example of integer overflow, as we reached and exceeded the maximum value that can be stored within the variable. As a consequence of integer overflow, the value stored inside the variable would restart from zero. Therefore, the value of 0 would be stored in the variable, instead of the requested value 256.

Integer underflow represents the opposite case to integer overflow, and occurs when the value to be stored inside the variable is smaller than the minimum value supported by the type of the variable.

In the case of integer underflow, the variable would restart storing the values in the variable beginning from the maximum values (in the case of a variable of the `uint8` type, the negative values would, in fact, be stored starting from the maximum allowed value of 255 downward).

Remediation of integer overflow and underflow

The safest method to prevent the occurrence of integer overflow and underflow is to use library functions that always verify the value obtained by performing mathematical operations on integer-type variables, comparing the result with the value we expected. The mathematical functions implemented by the OpenZeppelin library (available at https://github.com/OpenZeppelin/openzeppelin-solidity) ensure the integrity of operations on integer variables, and therefore should always be used when calculations are needed within the smart contract's instructions.

In the following section, we will show some examples of smart contract source code developed with Solidity, affected by the integer overflow vulnerability.

Overflow example code

We will now see some simple examples of integer overflow within smart contracts, and their possible fixes. The examples we show can be run and tested using the Remix **integrated development environment (IDE)**, available at https://remix.ethereum.org.

In the following code, we have developed a smart contract to receive and accumulate funds using the contract_balance variable, defined with the uint integer type.

An overflow example can be seen in the following code block:

```
pragma solidity 0.4.24;

contract Overflow_Example {
    uint public contract_balance = 0;

    function addFundsToBalance(uint256 funds) public {
        contract_balance += funds;
    }
}
```

Let's now analyze the source code details:

The addFundsToBalance() function accepts numeric values stored in the funds temporary variable, defined as the uint256 integer type.

The uint256 integer type may contain numeric values greater than those that can be represented within the contract_balance variable, defined as the uint integer type.

Therefore, the `addFundsToBalance()` function, by accumulating increasing amounts, can determine the integer overflow of the `contract_balance` variable.

A possible remedy aimed at preventing integer overflow is the different implementation of the `addFundsToBalance()` function, which is shown in the following example of an overflow being fixed:

```
pragma solidity 0.4.24;

contract Overflow_Fixed {
    uint public contract_balance = 0;

    function addFundsToBalance(uint256 funds) public {
        contract_balance = secure_add(contract_balance, funds);
    }

    function secure_add(uint256 balance, uint256 fund) internal pure
returns (uint256) {
        uint256 sum = balance + fund;

        require(sum >= balance);

        return sum;
    }
}
```

Instead of accumulating increasing values directly inside the `contract_balance` variable, as in the previous case, the `addFundsToBalance()` function now calls a specialized function: the `secure_add()` function. This function verifies that the result of the sum of the values is always greater than—or at least, equal to—the current value of the destination variable, preventing—in this case—the possibility of integer overflow. Similar examples can be developed to prevent cases of integer underflow, following the same logic shown before.

In the following section, we will see how it is possible to carry out a **Denial of Service (DoS)** attack by exploiting integer overflow within iterative instructions such as loops.

DoS using loops and overflow

We will now see how it is possible for an attacker to exploit the integer overflow vulnerability within iterative instructions represented by `for` loops, to achieve a DoS compromise.

First, let's define a contract called `ManagePayments`, which uses the `Payment` data structure to store payments received, as follows:

```solidity
pragma solidity ^0.4.24;

contract ManagePayments {

    struct Payment {
        address addr;
        uint amount;
    }

    Payment[] payments;

    function addPayment() public payable {
        Payment memory payment = Payment({
            addr: msg.sender,
            amount: msg.value
        });

        payments.push(payment);
    }

    function getPayment(uint id) public view returns (address, uint) {
        Payment memory payment = payments[id];
        return (payment.addr, payment.amount);
    }

}
```

The `addPayment()` function archives the payments received and stores the data within instances of the `Payment` structure. Those instances are then queued in the `payments` variable, defined as an array of `Payment` structures.

In the following section, we will show an example of a buggy smart contract, vulnerable to DoS attacks.

A buggy smart contract

As we said in Chapter 6, *Decentralized Apps and Smart Contracts*, the use of Turing-complete programming languages such as Solidity in the development of smart contracts can determine the occurrence of bugs within the source code. These bugs are due to the presence of conditional and iterative instructions, allowed by Turing-complete languages. In turn, bugs within iterative instructions such as `for` loops can result in DoS compromises, which can be quite insidious and difficult to prevent.

In the following example, we will show the `BuggyManagePayments` contract:

```solidity
pragma solidity ^0.4.24;

contract BuggyManagePayments {

    struct Payment {
        address addr;
        uint amount;
    }

    Payment[] payments;

    function addPayment() public payable {
        Payment memory payment = Payment({
            addr: msg.sender,
            amount: msg.value
        });

        payments.push(payment);
    }


    function getPayment(uint id) public view returns (address, uint) {
        Payment memory payment = payments[id];
        return (payment.addr, payment.amount);
    }

    // buggy function
    function sendPayments() public {
        for(uint8 c = 0; c < payments.length; c++) {
            payments[c].addr.transfer(payments[c].amount);
        }
    }

}
```

The contract is affected by two important bugs, due to the incorrect implementation of the for loop within the sendPayments() function. First, the for loop uses the c local variable, defined of type uint8 as the counter variable. As we know from the previous considerations, the maximum value that a variable of type uint8 can assume is 255. Therefore, this variable is susceptible to overflowing in the event that the payments array reaches and exceeds the length of 255 (represented by the payments.length value).

As a consequence of integer overflow, the index of the for loop would start again from 0 and would begin to transfer the payments already made previously. Furthermore, since there is no predefined limit to the length that the payments array can assume (this can, theoretically, be infinite), it could potentially exceed the allowed limits in terms of gas units. This would determine the conditions for a possible DoS exploitation in the sendPayments() function.

In the following section, we will see how to fix our buggy smart contract.

Fixing the buggy smart contract

To resolve the bugs found in the example smart contract, we need to make changes in the for loop within the sendPayments() function.

The following example shows the correct version of the sendPayments() function:

```
uint256 nextPayment;

function sendPayments() public {
    uint256 c = nextPayment;

    while (c < payments.length &amp;&amp; gasleft() > 100000) {
      payments[c].addr.transfer(payments[c].amount);
      c++;
    }

    nextPayment = c;
}
```

In the sendPayments() function, we have defined the c local variable (used as a counter within the for loop) with the integer type uint256, which can store values up to $2^{256} - 1$, thus preventing the possibility of integer overflow. Furthermore, we have also prevented the possibility of a DoS by establishing a limit in terms of gas units, adding the gasleft() > 100000 condition within the for loop.

The following code block shows the complete listing of the fixed contract:

```solidity
pragma solidity ^0.4.24;

contract CorrectManagePayments {

    struct Payment {
        address addr;
        uint amount;
    }

    Payment[] payments;

    function addPayment() public payable {
        Payment memory payment = Payment({
            addr: msg.sender,
            amount: msg.value
        });

        payments.push(payment);
    }


    function getPayment(uint id) public view returns (address, uint) {
        Payment memory payment = payments[id];
        return (payment.addr, payment.amount);
    }

    uint256 nextPayment;

    function sendPayments() public {
        uint256 c = nextPayment;

        while (c < payments.length &amp;&amp; gasleft() > 100000) {
          payments[c].addr.transfer(payments[c].amount);
          c++;
        }

        nextPayment = c;
    }

}
```

In the following section, we will address another fairly common vulnerability, known as a re-entrancy attack.

Re-entrancy attack

A re-entrancy attack constitutes one of the first bugs found on the Ethereum platform and consists of the possibility of repeatedly invoking certain functions defined within a smart contract, without waiting for the termination of previous calls. Because of its peculiarity in allowing the repeated invocation of functions, the re-entrancy attack is also known as a recursive call attack. By exploiting this type of bug, an attacker is in fact able to illicitly subtract all the funds available in a contract simply by making multiple invocations of the same function, causing unwanted results with respect to the expected behavior of the contract.

In the following example code, we compare two different versions of the same `withdraw()` function, one affected by the re-entrancy bug, while the other isn't:

```
// buggy withdraw function
function buggy_withdraw(uint amount) public{
  if (credit[msg.sender] >= amount) {
    require(msg.sender.call.value(amount)());
    credit[msg.sender] -= amount;
  }
}

// fixed withdraw function
function fixed_withdraw(uint amount) public {
  if (credit[msg.sender] >= amount) {
    credit[msg.sender] -= amount;
    require(msg.sender.call.value(amount)());
  }
}
```

Let's now analyze the source code details.

In the case of the `buggy_withdraw()` function, the low-level call to the `msg.sender.call.value(amount)()` method allows funds to be transferred to the address that made the function call. By repeatedly calling the `buggy_withdraw()` function, it is possible to illicitly subtract all the funds, until the gas unit of the contract is exhausted. This is possible because the contract allows calls to the `msg.sender.call.value(amount)()` method to be made repeatedly, before the status of the `credit[msg.sender]` variable is verified, which occurs only upon completion of the call to the `buggy_withdraw()` function.

In this way, an attacker can bypass the `credit[msg.sender]> = amount` condition check, depleting the funds left in the contract. To prevent a re-entrancy attack, it is advisable to use the `transfer()` method instead of the low-level invocation of the `call()` method. Alternatively, it is necessary to check the value assumed by the status variables (such as the `credit[msg.sender]` variable) before invoking the `call()` method.

 The `fixed_withdraw()` version of the contract does just that: it updates the value of the `credit[msg.sender]` variable before invoking the `msg.sender.call.value(amount)()` method.

After having introduced the main vulnerabilities affecting smart contracts, we are now able to analyze the main attacks that have been carried out on the Ethereum platform in the recent past.

In the following sections, we will analyze the famous **Decentralized Autonomous Organization (DAO)** and Parity attacks.

Smart contract attack examples

We will now analyze two of the main smart contract attacks performed on the Ethereum platform: the DAO attack and the Parity attack. Due to the DAO attack, carried out in June 2016, attackers were able to illegally subtract an amount of funds estimated at between 70 and 150 million USD, while with the Parity attack carried out in July 2017, they subtracted an amount of 30 million USD from Parity's multi-signature wallet.

So, let's start our analysis with the DAO attack, which is examined in the following section.

Analyzing the DAO attack

To carry out the DAO attack, the attacker exploited some bugs present in the original version of the `splitDAO` function, whose Solidity code is shown in the `DAO.sol` listing, available at `https://github.com/slockit/DAO/blob/v1.0/DAO.sol`.

In the following code, we report an extract of that code listing:

```
function splitDAO() {

    ...

    uint fundsToBeMoved = (balances[msg.sender] *
```

```
    p.splitData[0].splitBalance) / p.splitData[0].totalSupply;

    if
(p.splitData[0].newDAO.createTokenProxy.value(fundsToBeMoved)(msg.sender)
== false)

    ...

    Transfer(msg.sender, 0, balances[msg.sender]);

    withdrawRewardFor(msg.sender);

    totalSupply -= balances[msg.sender];

    balances[msg.sender] = 0;

    paidOut[msg.sender] = 0;

    return true;

}
```

By analyzing the source code of the `splitDAO()` function, we can easily verify the presence of a vulnerability consisting of issuing re-entrancy calls to the `Transfer()` and `withdrawRewardFor()` methods. The possibility of making these re-entrancy calls is due to the fact that the updating of the `totalSupply`, `balances[msg.sender]`, and `paidOut[msg.sender]` state variables occurs only at the end of the `splitDAO()` function. In fact, they take place after the invocation of the `Transfer(msg.sender, 0, balances[msg.sender])` and the `withdrawRewardFor(msg.sender)` statements.

In this way, an attacker can carry out a re-entrancy call attack, and consequently exhaust all available resources, stealing illicitly (and recursively) all the funds available in the contract.

Without waiting for the `splitDAO()` function to finish, the updates of the status variables (necessary to carry out the checks provided in the `if` condition) cannot take place, and the re-entrancy calls can be successfully performed.

In the next section, we'll analyze the Parity attack.

The Parity attack

To understand the vulnerability that led to the Parity attack, we will now show an example of a vulnerable contract that imitates the original Parity wallet code in a deliberately simplified form.

The `ParityVulnerableWallet` contract source code is shown in the following code block:

```
pragma solidity ^0.4.24;

contract ParityVulnerableWallet {

    address owner;

    function setOwner(address usr) {
        owner = usr;
    }

    function withdraw(uint funds) {
        if (msg.sender == owner) {
            owner.transfer(funds);
        }
    }

}
```

The contract defines an `owner` property, in which the contract owner's address is stored. Ideally, only the contract owner can withdraw funds from the contract by invoking the `withdraw()` function, which verifies that the sender's address matches that of the `owner`. However, the contract has an important vulnerability, represented by the `setOwner()` function, which allows the value contained in the `owner` variable to be updated by assigning any address passed in the `usr` parameter.

The `setOwner()` function should therefore only be visible within the contract, and callable only by the contract constructor. Due to its flawed definition, however, the `setOwner()` function can potentially be called from outside the contract, by any user or other smart contracts. The address contained in the `owner` variable can, therefore, be overwritten by substituting it with the attacker's own address. The attacker can consequently invoke the `withdraw()` function, thus illegally withdrawing funds from the contract, as happened in July 2017 with the Parity wallet attack.

In the following section, we see how to prevent the most common vulnerabilities that give rise to attacks on smart contracts.

Preventing smart contract attacks

We have seen how many attacks on smart contracts are often due to bugs contained within the source code. To prevent the occurrence of these bugs, it is thus appropriate to use specialized library functions that help the developer in the safe implementation of the most common functions. One of these libraries is the `SafeMath` library of the `OpenZeppelin` package (available at `https://github.com/OpenZeppelin/openzeppelin-solidity`).

By using the `SafeMath` library, it is possible to prevent bugs such as integer overflows and underflows.

In the following example, we show an excerpt of the implementation of the `add()` function offered by the `SafeMath` library:

```
pragma solidity ^0.4.24;

library SafeMath {

...

 /**
 * @dev Function to add two numbers
 */
 function add(uint256 a, uint256 b)
 internal pure returns (uint256 c) {
    c = a + b;
    assert(c >= a);
    return c;
 }

...

 }
```

Instead of implementing our functions—which may contain bugs—from scratch, we can therefore safely use the mathematical functions offered by libraries such as `SafeMath`. In addition to the use of specialized libraries, it is possible to resort to specific tools that help in identifying vulnerabilities within the source code and bytecode of smart contracts.

In the following sections, we will see the main tools for analyzing smart contract vulnerabilities.

Analyzing smart contracts for security

Various tools are freely available that help us analyze the vulnerability of smart contracts, the use of which is recommended both in the development and testing phases.

We will consider a couple of the most popular analysis tools, such as the following:

- **Mythril**: A security analysis tool for EVM bytecode, which can find security vulnerabilities in smart contracts. The tool is available at `https://github.com/ConsenSys/mythril`.

- **Securify**: A static and fully automated analyzer tool that scans the source code and generates a vulnerability report. The tool is available online at`https://securify.chainsecurity.com/`.

In the following sections, we will see more closely the functionality of these tools, starting with Mythril.

Analyzing smart contracts with Mythril

Mythril is a security analysis tool for EVM bytecode that can detect the most common smart contract vulnerabilities, such as integer overflows and underflows. It can detect security vulnerabilities for EVM-compatible blockchains (such as Ethereum, Quorum, VeChain, **Rootstock** (**RSK**), and TRON). Mythril is not aimed at discovering issues in the business logic of an application, and it is not able to explore all possible states of a program, as it uses symbolic execution to detect security vulnerabilities.

Let's take a look at the steps involved in this process:

1. To install Mythril from PyPI, just run the following command:

   ```
   pip3 install mythril
   ```

2. To start analyzing smart contracts in Solidity source format, just issue the following command:

   ```
   myth analyze <solidity-source-file>
   ```

3. We can also analyze contracts by simply passing their address to the tool, as follows:

```
myth analyze -a <contract-address>
```

4. The following code snippet shows an example execution of Mythril on the KillBilly contract (available at https://gist.github.com/b-mueller/ 2b251297ce88aa7628680f50f177a81a#file-killbilly-sol):

```
myth analyze killbilly.sol
```

5. Upon execution, the tool prints the following output on the screen:

```
==== Unprotected Selfdestruct ====
SWC ID: 106
Severity: High
Contract: KillBilly
Function name: commencekilling()
PC address: 354
Estimated Gas Usage: 574 - 999
The contract can be killed by anyone.
Anyone can kill this contract and withdraw its balance to an
arbitrary address.
--------------------
In file: killbilly.sol:22

selfdestruct(msg.sender)


--------------------
Transaction Sequence:

Caller: [CREATOR], data: [CONTRACT CREATION], value: 0x0
Caller: [ATTACKER], function: killerize(address), txdata:
0x9fa299ccbebebebebebebebebebebedeadbeefdeadbeefdeadbeefdeadbeefd
eadbeef, value: 0x0
Caller: [ATTACKER], function: activatekillability(), txdata:
0x84057065, value: 0x0
Caller: [ATTACKER], function: commencekilling(), txdata:
0x7c11da20, value: 0x0
```

As we can see, Mythril has successfully spotted the KillBilly contract as a suicidal contract.

Let's now see how to analyze smart contracts with Securify.

Analyzing smart contracts with Securify

Securify is a security scanner for Ethereum smart contracts that implements context-sensitive static analysis.

The tool can analyze smart contracts written in Solidity version >= 0.5.8 and is able to successfully spot the following vulnerabilities contemplated in the SWC Registry:

ID	Pattern name	Severity	Slither ID	SWC ID
1	TODAmount	Critical	-	SWC-114
2	TODReceiver	Critical	-	SWC-114
3	TODTransfer	Critical	-	SWC-114
4	UnrestrictedWrite	Critical	-	SWC-124
5	RightToLeftOverride	High	rtlo	SWC-130
6	ShadowedStateVariable	High	shadowing-state, shadowing-abstract	SWC-119
7	UnrestrictedSelfdestruct	High	suicidal	SWC-106
8	UninitializedStateVariable	High	uninitialized-state	SWC-109
9	UninitializedStorage	High	uninitialized-storage	SWC-109
10	UnrestrictedDelegateCall	High	controlled-delegatecall	SWC-112
11	DAO	High	reentrancy-eth	SWC-107
12	ERC20Interface	Medium	erc20-interface	-
13	ERC721Interface	Medium	erc721-interface	-
14	IncorrectEquality	Medium	incorrect-equality	SWC-132
15	LockedEther	Medium	locked-ether	-
16	ReentrancyNoETH	Medium	reentrancy-no-eth	SWC-107
17	TxOrigin	Medium	tx-origin	SWC-115

Securify and SWC Registry reference table

This diagram shows the SWC vulnerabilities that are covered by Securify.

To install Securify, we need to meet the following prerequisites:

- **Solc**: Install the Solidity compiler, available at `https://solidity.readthedocs.io/en/v0.5.10/installing-solidity.html`.
- **Soufflé**: Install Soufflé (available at `https://souffle-lang.github.io/install`), following the instructions you can find at `https://souffle-lang.github.io/download.html`

- **Graphviz**: Install the Graphviz reports library, available at `https://www.graphviz.org/download/`.
- **Python** version 3.7.

Once the prerequisites are met, we can install Securify by setting up the Python virtual environment, as follows:

1. From the project's root folder, just execute the following command:

```
virtualenv --python=/usr/bin/python3.7 venv
```

2. To activate the virtual environment just created, simply run the following command:

```
source venv/bin/activate
```

3. We can now analyze the source code of a contract by issuing the following command:

```
securify <contract_source>.sol
```

4. If the contract we want to analyze is deployed on the blockchain, we can pass to Securify the contract address and the API key obtained from `etherscan.io`, as follows:

```
securify <contract_address> --from-blockchain [--key <key-file>]
```

5. We can also analyze a contract by specifying the severity levels of interest, as follows:

```
securify <contract_source>.sol [--include-severity Severity1
Severity2]
```

```
securify <contract_source>.sol [--exclude-severity Severity1
Severity2]
```

These examples conclude our analysis of smart contract vulnerabilities.

Summary

In this chapter, we have analyzed some of the most common vulnerabilities affecting smart contracts. We have understood how the bugs present in the source code can have disastrous consequences on smart contracts, such as the ones experienced with the famous DAO and Parity wallet attacks. Preventing the onset of bugs within source code is, therefore, of fundamental importance. To this end, specialized libraries such as `OpenZeppelin` can be used in the development phase of smart contracts. Equally important is to conduct a vulnerability analysis using specialized tools such as Mythril and Securify, which help the developer in both the implementation and testing phases of smart contracts.

After having widely analyzed the vulnerabilities of DApps and smart contracts, in the next chapter, we will discover how it is possible to exploit the blockchain as an attack vector.

Section 4: Preserving Data Integrity and Privacy

4

In this section, you will be introduced to blockchain issues, such as GDPR and anti-laundering law compliance, that occur due to user anonymity and privacy, as well as the potential misuse of blockchain to perform anonymous attacks.

This section comprises the following chapters:

- Chapter 8, *Exploiting Blockchain as an Attack Vector*
- Chapter 9, *Analyzing Privacy and GDPR Compliance Issues*

8
Exploiting Blockchain as an Attack Vector

In this chapter, we will analyze possible misuses of blockchain that lead to potential attacks on data integrity, identity theft, and the spreading of malware by leveraging blockchain features. We will learn how attackers can leverage blockchain to store illicit data and whether or not illicit data may be erased from the blockchain. We'll also discuss controversial topics such as anonymity and identity theft within blockchain and cryptocurrencies. We will also show how blockchain can be leveraged to spread malicious software such as malware.

In particular, in this chapter, we will deal with the following topics:

- Storing illicit data in the blockchain
- Preserving anonymity in the blockchain
- Dealing with identity theft
- Spreading malware with Blockchain

Let's now begin with the following section, learning how illicit data can be stored in the blockchain.

Storing illicit data in the blockchain

Much of the attraction of the blockchain is undeniably due to the fact that it represents a tamper-proof public ledger. This feature has contributed to the growing trust associated with technology such as blockchain, which aims to guarantee robustness, transparency, and the reliability of transactions. It is no coincidence that various uses of blockchain technology have been hypothesized and implemented over time, ranging from financial transactions to identity management, to the supply chain.

The diffusion of smart contracts testifies to the growing interest in the use of the blockchain to ensure the transfer of assets and property rights in a safe way, thereby preventing the possibility of fraud. The prevention of the possibility of fraud in transactions is associated precisely with the public and distributed nature of the blockchain ledger. Although the public and distributed nature of the blockchain constitutes an undeniable disincentive to the interpretation of fraud in transactions, however, technology alone is not sufficient to prevent possible misuses.

In this chapter, with the term blockchain, we will refer to Bitcoin's blockchain, which represents the public blockchain par excellence. We will see how it is possible to store illegal data even on this type of blockchain.

 In fact, current technology can only trace the presence of data, guaranteeing its integrity, but it is not able to discriminate and prevent the storage of data of an illicit nature and origin. Not only that: the unchangeable nature of the ledger ends up being a problem, rather than an advantage, in the event that illegal data is stored.

An attacker could, therefore, decide to exploit the blockchain to store illicit data inside it (both in a clear and in an encrypted form), taking advantage of the characteristics of immutability and the availability of the blockchain itself. It has already happened in the past, with the advent of peer-to-peer (P2P) networks, when dishonest users got rid of compromising data, temporarily deleting it from their computers, to store it on the shared filesystem, in an attempt to evade police checks. If necessary, the data could be recovered by downloading it from the shared filesystem of the peer-to-peer network.

Unlike traditional peer-to-peer networks, though, the blockchain guarantees that no one can erase the data stored in it, including illegal data. The presence of illegal data within the blockchain, as we will see shortly, can expose all users to possible responsibilities for the simple fact of holding (even involuntarily and without being aware of it) a copy of such data inside their machines.

In the following section, we will see in more detail how it is possible to store illegal data within the blockchain.

Storing illicit data on Bitcoin's blockchain

The ability to store illegal data on the blockchain is due to the fact that it can be used to store not only data relating to financial transactions carried out in Bitcoin but also data and information of various kinds. Although, in fact, the blockchain was designed primarily to store transactions carried out through cryptocurrencies, it can also be used to record various types of data in an unchangeable way, such as texts, messages, images, and more. The possibility of archiving non-financial data has given rise to a whole series of further uses of blockchain technology, such as digital notarization, but has also allowed the possibility of using the blockchain for illicit purposes.

One of the first pieces of research conducted in this field dates back to 2018 and gave rise to a paper entitled *A Quantitative Analysis of the Impact of Arbitrary Blockchain Content on Bitcoin*, by Roman Matzutt, Jens Hiller, Martin Henze, Jan Henrik Ziegeldorf, Dirk Müllmann, Oliver Hohlfeld, and Klaus Wehrle (the paper is available at `https://roman-matzutt.de/publication/2018-fc-matzutt-bitcoin-contents/`). This research revealed the presence, already as of the date of publication of the paper, of a significant amount of non-financial data of various kinds, including illicit data, stored on Bitcoin's blockchain.

Let's now examine the main types of illegal data detected by the aforementioned research:

- **Illicit data comprising copyright violations**: Among the illegal data found on the blockchain, there were seven files whose publication violated copyright laws, as well as software to violate DVD copy protection. In addition, a leaked RSA private key and a firmware secret key were also found.
- **Illicit data affecting privacy**: Some of the files found included information processed in violation of the privacy protection rules. These files revealed private chats or images related to individuals' private lives. Other files exposed personal information, such as phone numbers, addresses, bank accounts, passwords, and multiple online identities. The unauthorized possession and processing of this information contravenes the current European privacy regulations (GDPR).
- **Illegal sexual content**: The research found the presence of illegal sexual content on Bitcoin's blockchain, including 274 links to websites, 142 of which referred to illegal sexual content stored on the deep web. The possession of such illegal content can expose even unaware users who download the local copy of the blockchain on their machine to criminal liability.

In the following section, we will examine the main methods used to store illicit data on the blockchain.

Storing illicit data on the blockchain through transactions

One of the main methods of storing illicit data on the blockchain is to take advantage of Bitcoin transactions. Usually, transactions are used to transfer funds between counterparties that are identified by their respective public-private key pairs. In Bitcoin, funds are unlocked using transaction script templates in order to prevent excessive transaction verification overheads. Even standard financial transactions can be used to insert non-financial data into the blockchain.

The different types of templates that can be used for standard financial transactions include the following:

- **Pay to public-key (P2PK)** and **pay to public-key hash (P2PKH) transactions**: With these types of transactions, it is possible to transfer funds to a counterparty identified by an address obtained from the recipient's private key.
- **Pay to script hash (P2SH) transactions**: The transfer of funds refers to a script, instead of keys.

To transfer arbitrary data using standard financial transactions, it is possible to replace the respective public keys and hash value scripts with arbitrary data. However, this option is expensive, since the replacement of valid receiver identifiers with arbitrary data determines the invalidity of the receiver identifiers. As a result, the transaction is discarded, and the funds used in the transaction are lost. However, P2SH input scripts can be published along with their redeem script, thus preventing the transaction from being discarded.

The miner nodes proceed, in fact, to verify the P2SH transactions even in cases where the redeem scripts are not template compliant, as long as the overall P2SH transactions are syntax compliant. It is also possible to use third-party services and tools to insert arbitrary content into the blockchain.

Usable services and tools include the following:

- **CryptoGraffiti**: A web service that transfers files on the blockchain making use of multiple P2PKH scripts within a single transaction (the web service is publicly available at `https://cryptograffiti.info/`).
- **Apertus**: This service allows file transfers by fragmenting content and making use of an arbitrary number of P2PKH scripts (the tool is available at `http://apertus.io/`).

The problem relating to the possibility of storing illegal data on the blockchain brings us back to the controversial theme of the possibility (as well as the opportunity) of deleting the data stored in the blockchain.

In the following section, we will see how to deal with the problem of deleting illegal data within Bitcoin's blockchain.

Erasing illicit data from the blockchain

As we said in the *Storing illicit data in the blockchain* section, the presence of illegal data within the blockchain also exposes the user who downloads a local copy of the transactions to their machine to criminal liability. Having the possibility to delete such illegal data is, therefore, a legitimate feature request, which would help users eliminate unwanted data, at least from the local copy they downloaded on their machines. How is it possible to reconcile this data deletion request with the requirement of the ledger's immutability, prescribed and respected by the blockchain?

A simple and direct method to globally delete the data previously entered within the blockchain is to make a hard fork. However, in public blockchains such as Bitcoin's, the realization of the hard fork presupposes the achievement of consensus among miners, users, and other network operators.

This consensus is notoriously difficult to achieve, especially if motivated by the request for the deletion of potentially controversial data. The problem with deleting illegal data must, therefore, be addressed in a more pragmatic way. Allowing the deletion of locally stored data for legal or ethical reasons is not only reasonable but contributes to maintaining a healthy blockchain ecosystem, increasing the presence of a large number of full nodes by reducing the risks of legal liabilities on individual operators and organizations.

Among the reasons that inhibit the deletion of blockchain data by local nodes, there is the assumption that this would imply permanently restricting nodes from participating in the blockchain in a full-node mode. In a recent study conducted by researchers M. Florian, S. Beaucamp, S. Henningsen, and B. Scheuermann, entitled *Erasing Data from Blockchain Nodes* (available at `https://arxiv.org/abs/1904.08901`), the authors questioned the commonly held opinion that data erasure is not possible for node operators in public blockchains like Bitcoin's.

The authors of the paper propose the adoption of a functionality-preserving local erasure (FPLE) approach. The FPLE approach also allows nodes operating in full-node mode to erase unwanted data by removing transaction data from the local storage, while continuing to store and validate other blockchain transactions. In other words, FPLE also allows blockchain's full nodes to delete locally stored data that's considered problematic, without the need to achieve a global consensus on the deletion of such data. The global erasure of data considered problematic would, in fact, be possible only by achieving the global consensus of the network.

Anyway, the deletion of locally stored data would not prevent FPLE from scaling to global erasure, with other nodes also adopting data deletion as well.

In the following section, we'll see how to erase data from Bitcoin's blockchain by leveraging the Bitcoind Erase tool.

Erasing data from Bitcoin's blockchain with Bitcoind Erase

To demonstrate the functionality of the FPLE approach, the authors of the paper prepared the Bitcoind Erase tool, freely available at `https://github.com/marfl/bitcoind-erase`. Bitcoind Erase represents a proof-of-concept implementation of Bitcoin's nodes operating in full mode. To understand how the FPLE approach works, we need to analyze the concept of local pruning.

Usually, pruning operations are carried out to reduce the storage needs of a network, by erasing older parts of the local copy of the blockchain, starting from a certain point in time.

 The FPLE approach constitutes an extension of the concept of pruning.

In the case of FPLE, individual data chunks representing unwanted data are deleted. To this end, FPLE allows individual nodes to mark the chunks of data that must be deleted, without the need to achieve global trust or coordination with the other nodes.

The chunks of data that have been marked for deletion are physically erased from the local storage, and references to erased data are also stored in a database, to distinguish erased data from non-existent data. One of the main problems to be addressed in FPLE consists of the pruning of data potentially relevant for validating future blocks, as unwanted data may, in fact, be inserted in potentially spendable transaction outputs.

In the event that there are validations based on erased data, erasing nodes ignore unconfirmed transactions whose validation depends on erased data. If, on the other hand, a transaction that depends on erased data should be included in the blockchain, the erasing nodes assume that the validation of the deleted data has been successfully completed. To demonstrate in concrete terms the operation of the FPLE approach on Bitcoin's blockchain, the Bitcoind Erase tool shows the cancellation of the transaction indicated in the `example_config.json` configuration file.

To launch the tool, you need to run the following command:

```
tool.py example_config.json
```

According to the experiments conducted by the authors of the proof of concept, it was possible to keep the full node synchronized with the blockchain, continuing to regularly validate the incoming blocks for over 2 months without the need for interventions.

In the following section, we will deal with another feature of the blockchain that is exploited (often wrongly) in pursuit of illegal activities: the alleged anonymity of Bitcoin transactions.

Preserving anonymity in the blockchain

Another of the characteristics that attracted attention to the blockchain is that relating to the alleged possibility of preserving the anonymity of participants in transactions, despite the presence of a public distributed ledger. We will now see where this anonymity claim originated, often wrongly considered among the advantages of using cryptocurrencies. To ensure the ownership of funds, transactions are digitally signed with the private key of the user who transfers the funds. Both the signature and the public key are thus included in the transaction, to allow anyone to verify that the funds transferred really belong to the sender.

The counterparties of a transaction are identified by their Bitcoin addresses, which correspond to their respective public keys. Although these public keys are associated with specific transactions, however, nobody is able to know for sure the true identity of the owners of the public keys associated with the Bitcoin addresses. Similar to what happens in the banking world, Bitcoin addresses can be compared to the IBAN codes associated with bank accounts. The mere knowledge of IBAN bank account codes does not reveal anything to us about their real owners. In the same way, by simply analyzing the transactions stored within the blockchain, it is not possible to obtain information relating to the cryptocurrency portfolios, nor to trace their real holders.

This feature led many to believe that Bitcoin transactions enjoyed a high degree of anonymization and that, therefore, bitcoin transactions could be used to carry out illegal activities (such as, for example, spreading ransomware and malicious software) in complete anonymity. However, it is possible to obtain information on the holders of Bitcoin addresses by correlating this information with those freely available on the web.

In fact, information on Bitcoin addresses can often be obtained by carefully analyzing resources available online. Bitcoin addresses can be associated with websites or social media accounts, which provide clues to the possible owners of these addresses.

As a demonstration that the anonymity of Bitcoin transactions actually constitutes a myth, in the following section, we will show a striking case of unmasking criminal activities conducted exclusively using Bitcoin transactions.

Bitcoin's anonymity myth

The use of Bitcoin is often associated with criminal activities, and therefore is viewed with suspicion, due to the publicly held opinion that Bitcoin can guarantee high levels of anonymity. For this reason, it is supposed to be the preferred means of payment for conducting illegal activities. The reality and investigative experiences have instead shown the opposite. As proof of the fact that the anonymity of Bitcoins is actually a myth, we will reference the Silk Road case, considered at the time to be the largest online illegal marketplace in the world.

Ross Ulbricht, considered the owner of Silk Road, and who was therefore investigated by the police authorities, defended himself by claiming that, in reality, he had only been the creator of the marketplace, which had subsequently been owned and managed by others. The defense of Ulbricht actually relied on the fact that the illicit transactions of the marketplace had been conducted using only Bitcoins, in the belief that this effectively protected the anonymity of the counterparties, and that therefore the transactions could not be traced back to the real operators.

Instead, the prosecutors were able to trace the illicit transactions carried out using Bitcoins to Ulbricht, providing incontrovertible proof of the transfer of over 700,000 Bitcoins from the marketplace directly to Ulbricht's Bitcoin wallet. This demonstrates the fact that Bitcoin transactions are far from anonymous, and that they can, on the contrary, assist investigative authorities in identifying culprits.

To understand how it is possible to trace the real identity of counterparties, in the following section, we will show how the public keys used in transactions can be associated with the identities of counterparties.

Public keys as identities

To carry out a Bitcoin transaction, each counterparty must be identifiable by means of a unique Bitcoin address, associated with the respective public key. This unique identifier is necessary to identify and distinguish the individual transactions registered in the ledger. Although the real identities of the holders of Bitcoin addresses are not registered within the blockchain, it is possible to trace them indirectly. In fact, it is sufficient for anyone who knows the real identity of a counterparty in a transaction to reveal (even involuntarily) this identity publicly, so as to put an end to anonymity.

The public keys used as Bitcoin addresses are therefore able to hide the real identity of their owners as long as these identities are not associated with further identification data. Instead of anonymity, it would, therefore, be more correct to speak of pseudoanonymity as Bitcoin addresses and the corresponding public keys work in the same way as pseudonyms – just think of the writers who use a nom de plume when publishing their books. Increasingly, to comply with anti-money laundering regulations, online retailers, exchanges, and other professional intermediaries operating in Bitcoins are asked to identify the real owners of cryptocurrencies.

In order to preserve a high degree of anonymity, the use of one-time public keys has therefore been suggested, as we will see in the following section.

One-time public keys and stealth addresses

The use of a new key pair for each Bitcoin transaction is also recommended in the Bitcoin white paper, although this is considered a security measure rather than a technique to guarantee anonymity. Stealth addresses consist of generating a one-time transaction using hashed one-time keys. This technique is adopted by the Monero cryptocurrency in hiding the recipient of a transaction, by associating it with a newly generated address and a secret key.

The use of different accounts, and their related one-time addresses specifically created to carry out individual transactions, presupposes that it is not possible (or that it is extremely difficult) to trace the identity of counterparties starting from blockchain transaction analysis.

What has been said so far leads us to analyze the anonymity of transactions, which is the subject of the following section.

Transaction anonymity

To ensure the anonymity of transactions, special tools have been introduced. Among these, one of the best known is CoinJoin. CoinJoin allows users interested in making collective payments to achieve anonymity by mixing together their payments in Bitcoins. This makes it more difficult to uniquely attribute payments to each individual. However, if a single individual uses CoinJoin to carry out several transactions in a short time frame, it is still possible to trace the transactions to the same subject with a high statistical reliability. In addition, the possibility of information leakages in transactions still allows you to trace the identity of the subjects who carried out the transactions, also through tools such as CoinJoins.

Often, these information leaks are due to the use of web trackers and digital cookies on websites. These tools send information to both search engines and social media, for marketing, analytics, and advertising purposes. Some web trackers may also disclose users' personal information (such as names and email addresses) to third-party services, and such information may be correlated in the identification of the counterparties of the transactions carried out in Bitcoins. In general, the **Open Sources Intelligence** (**OSInt**) activities carried out by government and investigative authorities are able to statistically relate publicly available information with that obtainable from Bitcoin transactions, to trace the real identities of owners.

In order to respond to the legitimate needs of protecting operators' anonymity and privacy, the introduction of digital coins specifically designed to protect users' privacy was therefore proposed.

In the following section, we will analyze the main privacy coins available.

Privacy coins

Zcash and Monero are among the most widely used digital coins commonly adopted to protect users' privacy. Zcash is able to hide sensitive information related to a transaction, such as the sender, the recipient, and the amount transferred. In the same way, Monero is able to obscure sensitive transaction data by using stealth addresses and random signatures obtained from the blockchain and inserted into transactions. In this way, it is not possible to easily trace which of the signatures really belongs to the sender of the transaction.

Even in the case of the use of privacy coins, the effective protection of privacy and anonymity is conditioned by compliance with increasingly stringent regulations, adopted nationally and internationally to combat money laundering, which are also applicable to professional operators in digital coins.

In the following sections, we will examine in more detail the issues related to the protection of personal identity using blockchain technology.

Dealing with identity theft

One of the most serious problems that immediately arose with the spread of the internet is that of the verification and protection of users' identities. One of the most widespread memes stated that, on the internet, nobody knows you're a dog (`https://en.wikipedia.org/wiki/On_the_Internet,_nobody_knows_you%27re_a_dog`). Being able to verify the real identity of online users is also necessary to prevent identity theft. Blockchain technology has therefore been considered by many to be an effective tool in verifying and protecting users' identity. Taking advantage of the same cryptographic validation techniques used in the blockchain to achieve data integrity, it is believed that even personal identity can also be effectively protected from identity theft attacks.

In the following section, we will go deeper into issues related to identity theft.

Stealing users identities

Identity theft represents one of the most worrying threats against private citizens, who are increasingly asked to use digital services to have access to services offered by public administrations.

With the pervasive diffusion of digital technologies, even in sectors such as health, the protection of personal identity is becoming increasingly decisive in protecting physical safety as well as economic assets from possible identity theft.

Possible attack scenarios regarding identity theft include the following:

- The theft of personal documents, such as a passport, social security number, or driver's license: Through the theft of documents certifying identity, it is possible to trace sensitive information such as credit cards and bank accounts. The same documents can be used to perform illegal activities by impersonating the identity of unaware victims (such as subscribing for loans on behalf of victims, and opening offshore bank accounts to carry out money laundering operations).
- Using victims' payment credentials to make (or even simulate) online purchases of items and services.
- Synthetic identity theft: This consists of mixing stolen information with other false information in order to create false identities to perform criminal activities.

In the future, with the spread of the **Internet of Things** (**IoT**) and the expansion of the attack surface that IoT makes possible, it will be easier than ever before for attackers to be able to steal confidential user information to perpetrate identity theft attacks.

In the following subsections, we will analyze the real advantages and possible limits of using the blockchain to prevent identity theft attacks.

Managing and protecting identity with blockchain

The use of blockchain technology is considered by many to be an effective remedy to manage and protect identity from possible attacks, thus preventing the possibility of identity theft or identity fraud. This belief is based on the fact that the distributed ledger represents a data archive, the fraudulent alteration of which is considered almost impossible. Taking advantage of this feature of immutability and the reliability of the ledger, it is believed that the blockchain can represent the solution to identity verification and authentication problems.

According to supporters of blockchain-based solutions, once identities are inserted into the blockchain, it would be practically impossible for attackers to overcome the protection offered by the use of advanced blockchain encryption. The blockchain would, therefore, represent a reliable source of identity verification, which other operators (both private and governmental) could also turn to in order to reliably verify the identity of their users. Furthermore, by introducing the concept of credential notarization, it would also be possible to verify the ownership of certificates and diplomas issued by universities to users, through the application of hashes on digital identities, which would act as electronic seals.

It would, therefore, be impossible to manipulate or alter certificates on which these electronic seals have been affixed by universities or other organizations, thus certifying the skills achieved by users. The user would also be able to verify who has access to their personal data and could authorize access only to certain trusted parties, restricting access only to personal data deemed strictly necessary. This would prevent the possibility of fraud based on identity theft from the start. Despite the enthusiasm that blockchain has gained in many industrial sectors, the reality is actually very different.

Unfortunately, blockchain technology alone cannot be considered the definitive solution to many current problems, including those concerning protection from identity theft attacks.

In the following section, we will see how effective blockchain technology is at preventing identity theft.

How effective is blockchain at preventing identity theft?

In this section, we are limiting our analysis to the real benefits that blockchain technology can offer to prevent identity theft attacks. Anyway, similar considerations can be drawn in general on the protection and reliable management of identity through blockchain-based solutions.

The major difficulties that arise in identity management have to do with two main steps:

1. Ensuring that identities are real and unique
2. Verifying the attribution of identities to legitimate owners

In the next subsection, we'll see how to deal with the requirement of ensuring real and unique identities.

Ensuring real and unique identities

The first requirement is essential in preventing synthetic identity theft attacks, in which identities are created by mixing real data with artfully faked information. To understand the impact of fake synthetic identities, it is estimated that over 80% of credit card fraud is attributable to synthetic identity attacks.

Actually, the blockchain does not provide any effective advantage in fulfilling the first requirement.

The blockchain merely registers identity data in the ledger, but is unable to ascertain its veracity at the origin, which is simply taken for granted.

Moreover, due to the immutability of the ledger, in the event that a fake synthetic identity is inserted into the blockchain, it would be very difficult to remove it.

In other words, as seen in the case of the blockchain as well, the **Garbage In-Garbage Out (GIGO)** principle applies, whereby the verification of the truthfulness of the identity at the origin must be carried out with means and procedures other than the blockchain.

The only subjects capable of ascertaining the veracity of identities are government bodies that issue identity cards, while the blockchain limits itself to taking the veracity of identities as acquired information.

Verifying the attribution of identities to legitimate owners

Once the veracity of an identity has been ascertained, the second step consists of verifying the attribution of the identity to the legitimate owner.

Again, using the blockchain offers few real benefits in identity verification.

In fact, the revolutionary aspect of blockchain in the field of cryptocurrencies such as Bitcoin consists precisely in the fact that there is no need to prove who we really are in order to use digital coins.

Each user is able to create as many accounts as they want, without being requested to reveal their identity or the overall number of accounts they hold to others. On the other hand, if the alleged greater reliability of the blockchain in the verification of identities goes back to the use of **public-private key cryptography** (**PKI**), it is sufficient to use the already existing tools and architectures that are based on PKI.

The reliability and efficiency of these architectures have already been tested over the years. Therefore, there is no need to resort to experimental blockchain-based solutions to manage critical information such as that associated with identities.

Finally, due to the fact that identity verification has already been carried out elsewhere, in the event that an attacker takes possession and full control of the identity of a real person, the blockchain would still not be able to prevent the attacker from exploiting the identity stolen. The possibility of inserting data of a different nature into the blockchain allows attackers to use the blockchain as a vector for spreading malicious software (malware).

In the following section, we will see how to exploit the blockchain to spread a particular type of malware, known as K-ary malware.

Spreading malware with blockchain

The possible presence of malware within Bitcoin's blockchain was confirmed by the aforementioned paper entitled *A Quantitative Analysis of the Impact of Arbitrary Blockchain Content on Bitcoin*.

Although the suspicious software detected within the blockchain by the researchers did not represent effective malware and therefore does not pose a real threat to data integrity, it nevertheless represents potential annoyances for users, as the installed antivirus software could prevent access to important blockchain files following the detection of suspicious signatures.

However, the possibility of exploiting the peculiar characteristics of the blockchain as an attack vector for spreading real malware was verified by a recently published paper, entitled *Developing a K-ary Malware Using Blockchain*, by Joanna Moubarak, Eric Filiol, and Maroun Chamoun (available at `https://arxiv.org/abs/1804.01488`), in which a particular type of malware is implemented, the k-ary malware, which exploits the blockchain as a privileged environment for its diffusion.

Before analyzing the results of the paper and understanding the specific characteristics of the k-ary malware, we must devote a few words to current malware, and to strategies adopted to evade the control of antivirus software.

Malware versus antivirus software

In this section, we'll analyze the features and strategies used respectively by malicious software and antivirus software. Let's start with the techniques commonly used by antivirus software to detect the presence of malware.

These techniques can be summarized as follows:

- **Static analysis**: Static analysis techniques try to detect the presence of malware without executing them. To this end, signature databases are used, in which the hash digest calculated on the previously detected malware is stored, and a static analysis is carried out on the characteristics of the executables deemed suspicious, involving library functions calls, strings contained in binary images, remote URLs, and so on.
- **Dynamic analysis**: Dynamic analysis techniques are based on the execution of suspicious executables within controlled environments, such as sandboxes, in order to understand their behavior. To this end, automated procedures for analyzing the behavior of executables are often used, which can also take advantage of machine learning for the early detection of possible threats.

To evade antivirus software checks, malware can adopt the following techniques:

- **Polymorphism**: With polymorphism, malware inserts some instructions that do not substantially change the overall behavior of the executable, but by modifying the signatures, it confuses antivirus software.
- **Payload encryption**: By encrypting the payload, the malware makes the detection activity more difficult.
- **Payload packing**: Applying compression techniques to the payload alters the malware's instruction sequence, thereby avoiding static detection techniques.

- **Anti-debugging**: Anti-debugging techniques are designed to prevent executables from running in controlled environments, making the dynamic analysis of malware more difficult.
- **Steganography**: Through steganography, malware is hidden inside apparently harmless files, such as videos, images, and PDFs.

Despite the use of advanced techniques in the realization of malware, most of it consists of single executable files, which, at most, can download updates of the payload from the internet once they are launched on the victims' machines. For antivirus software, it is therefore only a matter of time before it is able to detect the presence of new malware and consequently update its signature databases. However, there is a category of malware that is capable of making it extremely difficult for antivirus software to detect its presence.

This category is known as K-ary malware and will be introduced in the following section.

Getting to know K-ary malware

Unlike common malware, whose malicious instructions are contained mainly within a single executable file, k-ary malware divides malicious instructions into separate k chunks, thus partitioning the code into k autonomous files. In this way, individual chunks contain seemingly harmless instructions and are not detected as suspicious by antivirus software. In practice, the segregation of the viral payload is applied in k-ary malware, by distributing it on k different autonomous units, which go undetected by antivirus software.

Based on the use of distinct k chunks, k-ary malware can be divided into two classes:

- **Class I**: The k-ary malware belonging to this category can use k chunks sequentially, without the need for the k files to be simultaneously present on the victim system.
- **Class II**: The k-ary malware belonging to this category can run k chunks in parallel. Therefore, the k files must be simultaneously present on the victims' system.

Particular considerations can be drawn from the analysis of the computational complexity of k-ary malware (please refer to the *Computational complexity* section in Chapter 3, *Blockchain Security Assumptions*). Indeed, it has been demonstrated (please refer to the paper *Malware of the future*, by E. Filiol, available at http://archive.hack.lu/2008/ Malware%20of%20the%20Future.pdf), that the detection of the presence of k-ary malware constitutes a problem belonging to the NP-complete complexity class.

As such, it cannot be solved by a Turing machine in polynomial time. Consequently, the detection of the presence of k-ary malware goes beyond the computational capabilities of common antivirus software.

In the following section, we will learn why blockchain is the ideal environment for the spread of k-ary malware.

Blockchain as the vector of choice for k-ary malware spreading

After having introduced the characteristics of k-ary malware and understood that the detection of its presence constitutes a problem that goes beyond the computational capabilities of common antivirus software, we are now able to comprehend the reasons why the blockchain is the ideal environment for spreading this type of malware.

In the development of k-ary malware, it is necessary to solve some problems concerning the identification of individual k chunks, and the problem of agreeing on the complexity of the cryptographic key generation. It is at this point that the blockchain comes into play. The individual k chunks of which the malware is composed can, in fact, be inserted and validated within the Bitcoin blockchain. In this way, the blockchain ensures that the individual k chunks belong to the same malware.

The blockchain thus allows you to retrieve multiple chunks of the k-ary malware, ensuring the authenticity and integrity of the individual chunks, and overcoming the problem of managing the generation of the encryption keys, which is delegated to the blockchain itself.

In this way, it is possible to spread undetectable malware by exploiting the architectural characteristics of the blockchain.

Summary

In this chapter, we explored the possibility of exploiting the blockchain as an attack vector. We saw that not only data of a different nature can be stored within the blockchain, but that this possibility also exposes unaware users to responsibility and liability. In similar cases, the immutability of the ledger can turn into a disadvantage, rather than an advantage, and we have seen what solutions can be adopted to eliminate illicit data from local nodes. We then dealt with some topics still considered controversial, such as the possibility of exploiting the blockchain to preserve the anonymity of users and transactions, and to guarantee users protection from possible identity theft attacks. Finally, we saw how it is possible to spread malware by exploiting the architectural peculiarities of the blockchain, making it extremely difficult for antivirus software to detect malicious software.

In the next chapter, we will deal with the compliance aspects of blockchain with the European privacy legislation (GDPR), an extremely relevant topic that represents the timely overall assessment of the security and privacy of blockchain technology.

Analyzing Privacy and GDPR Compliance Issues

9

This chapter analyzes the potential privacy issues arising with the adoption of blockchain, particularly in terms of privacy law compliance. We will address some of the most controversial use cases and scenarios, such as those involving the protection of sensitive data stored in blockchains, ensuring the privacy of sensitive healthcare data, and protecting sensitive data accessed from IoT devices. Finally, we'll learn how to manage and deploy blockchain technology in order to comply with the European Union's **General Data Protection Regulation** (**GDPR**) privacy law.

The topics covered in the chapter are as follows:

- Preserving sensitive data in a blockchain
- Leveraging blockchain for healthcare
- Improving IoT security with blockchain
- Reconciling blockchain with the GDPR

In the next section, we will see how to protect sensitive data stored within a blockchain.

Preserving sensitive data in a blockchain

One of the most delicate matters that must be assessed in relation to compliance with privacy protection regulations concerns storing sensitive data within a blockchain. Choosing which information to actually store within a blockchain is therefore one of the fundamental decisions that needs to be made.

The data that is published on a blockchain is in fact accessible to all the nodes participating in the network. This is true both in public blockchains, where there are no restrictions on access to the ledger, and in permissioned blockchains, although in the latter case access to data is allowed only to known and trusted counterparts.

In the next section, we will examine what data must actually be stored within a blockchain.

What data should be stored on a blockchain

Although in theory a blockchain allows any type of data to be stored inside it, this does not mean that it is appropriate to proceed with the direct storage of all types of data. There are several reasons to advise against using blockchains as shared storage. First, the data within a blockchain is stored in the form of transactions. Therefore, storing large amounts of data involves significant costs, since transaction fees are commensurate with the size of the data entered within the transaction.

Furthermore, the data stored within a blockchain should be only that which does not require frequent changes, since by definition a blockchain does not allow modification of data that's already stored. The only way to update the state of the already-archived data is to add new transactions containing the changes made to the state of the data.

Another deterrent is that blockchain is not the best technology for managing transactions quickly and in real time. On the contrary, as we know from Chapter 3, *Blockchain Security Assumptions*, to ensure the security and integrity of the ledger it is necessary to wait for a minimum number of block confirmations before the transaction is actually included in the blockchain.

But there is an even more stringent motivation that prevents the storage of some particular categories of data within a blockchain. In compliance with the Privacy Rule of the **Health Insurance Portability and Accountability Act** (**HIPAA**), no sensitive medical information should be stored on a blockchain.

This is why it is essential to store data and information that cannot be directly inserted into a blockchain in off-chain storage.

In the following section, we will see how to store sensitive data off-chain.

Storing sensitive data off-chain

We have already encountered the problem of dealing with data privacy in the *Hyperledger transaction privacy* section of `Chapter 5`, *Securing Hyperledger Fabric*. In general, whenever it is necessary to manage sensitive personal data through the blockchain or **distributed ledger technologies** (**DLTs**), it is possible to store such data in off-chain mode, that is to say, within a traditional database. The data thus stored can be protected by encryption, while only references (in the form of hashes) to such data are inserted within the blockchain.

This would also preclude the need for transaction confirmations, consequently improving the performance of the blockchain. In theory, the off-chain storage method would also allow the exercise of some of the rights enshrined in the GDPR. The storage of personal data in off-chain mode would in fact allow the modification and deletion of personal data, in compliance with Articles 16 (which provides for the exercise of the right to rectification) and 17 (which establishes the right to be forgotten) of the GDPR.

However, the problem of managing the hash references that are stored within the blockchain, which would be linked to modified or even deleted data, would remain.

In the next section we will learn more about the use of blockchain in the particularly delicate sector of healthcare, in which the protection of sensitive personal data constitutes a mission-critical task.

Leveraging blockchain for healthcare

The sharing of medical information between various organizations while ensuring the security, integrity, and privacy of health data represents one of the most significant problems in the digital healthcare field. It is therefore increasingly proposed to adopt blockchain technology in order to exploit the characteristics of immutability and integrity inherent in blockchain when sharing data between different operators.

In fact, in the healthcare domain it must be ensured that access to patient's health data is reserved only for authorized subjects in order to protect not only patients' privacy, but also their safety. Healthcare organizations are also required to comply with both the GDPR rules and the Privacy Rule of the HIPAA of 1996.

In the following section, we see how blockchain technology helps protect healthcare data.

Protecting healthcare data with blockchain

Among the advantages offered by the adoption of blockchain technology in the healthcare sector, there is the possibility of storing and sharing health data while guaranteeing its integrity. One of the main features of blockchain is that it can store information immutably. To this feature must also be added the guarantee to prevent access to data by unauthorized persons. A possible data breach would expose healthcare organizations to strict legal ramifications, as well as jeopardizing patient privacy and safety.

One way to allow access to shared data in a secure way by checking the respective permissions assigned to different operators could be to use smart contracts. By means of a smart contract, the patient would be able to receive notifications about who is accessing their health data at any given moment, thus allowing them to decide whether or not to authorize access to the data.

In the following section, we will examine what features a smart contract should provide in order to safely manage sensitive personal data in the healthcare sector.

Managing healthcare data with smart contracts

In the management of shared medical data, healthcare organizations must be able to guarantee the following:

- Data integrity
- Data confidentiality
- Data protection

Blockchain technology, with its tamper-proof nature, directly preserves the integrity of data. Ensuring the confidentiality of data means, first of all, preventing the possibility of unauthorized access to data. A solution must be implemented in order to authenticate those authorized to access the data. Personal medical data will therefore be protected by using encryption. Since medical data can be shared between different operators, the requirements set out at the beginning of this section can be respected by adopting a decentralized solution in the form of DApps, mainly as a smart contract (we examined DApps and smart contracts in Chapter 6, *Decentralized Apps and Smart Contracts*).

To fully understand the features implemented by the hypothetical smart contract, we can imagine the following scenario. First of all, the smart contract must identify the various operators authorized to access the shared medical data. Doctors, hospitals, health insurance companies, drug suppliers, and, of course, the patient themselves can be considered authorized operators. Obviously, the various authorized operators will be able to access the medical data with their own authorization levels. Authorized operators will be identified by their respective public-private key pairs. The information is managed in the form of blockchain transactions through the smart contract, which verifies the operators and the operations allowed to them on the data.

Once the verification has been successfully carried out, the transaction is inserted into the ledger, and all participants receive the updated copy of the blockchain, thus ensuring the integrity and immutability of the transactions.

Another sector in which the protection of sensitive data is becoming increasingly important is that of the **Internet of Things (IoT)**. In the following section, we will explore how using a blockchain can help solve IoT security problems.

Improving IoT security with blockchain

IoT is becoming increasingly important in the development of next-generation technological solutions. However, there are challenges commensurate with the increase in development opportunities, especially in terms of security and privacy. The distinctive feature of IoT is the ability to connect different types of device to each other, not limited to traditional computers, but also objects of common use, such as appliances, sensors, cameras, televisions, and even people and other living beings.

Each device is identified on IoT by a unique identifier. Within IoT, each device is able to independently establish communications with other devices based on different communication protocols: human-to-machine, machine-to-machine, and so on. Establishing communications automatically and pervasively between the different devices within IoT has the consequence that the potential attack surface grows dramatically.

The challenges of IoT security therefore consist not only of protecting devices and networks, but also the flow of information that is exchanged in the communications between the various devices. Ensuring the security and confidentiality of information is therefore of critical importance for the future development of IoT. To understand how IoT can benefit from the adoption of blockchain technology, we must first analyze the security threats that may arise in the specific context of IoT.

We therefore analyze the main security threats facing IoT in the following section.

IoT security threats

Security threats in the IoT sector are due to several factors. First, given its experimental nature, IoT designers focus mainly on functionality rather than on security. In other words, manufacturers of IoT devices and solutions have a greater interest in making and putting their products on the market as soon as possible, consequently reducing the time (and cost) of design and the verification of security issues. Other problems then arise in the interfacing of IoT devices with legacy software and devices, which were not originally designed to be connected to other appliances on the network, or were simply not designed for IoT. It is therefore not uncommon to find, within these legacy devices, weak default passwords that had been set assuming that access to the device would take place exclusively on site and not through remote connections.

Other problems are due to the poor hardware equipment of the devices (just think, for example, of RFID tags), which do not allow the implementation of strong security protocols based on cryptography due to the high computational load that they entail. Another aspect that makes the implementation of security solutions difficult is the lack of shared standards in the design of IoT appliances. All this translates into an increased surface of attack, which implies an assumption of responsibility in ensuring the security of IoT, which involves not only organizations but also end users. As evidence of the possible negative repercussions due to the larger attack surface of IoT, there are already many cases of security breaches that have occurred.

Attackers often exploit the weaknesses of IoT devices in order to spread through underlying networks. One of the first and most striking cases that can be traced back to an IoT security breach is the famous Stuxnet malware, which spread from a USB thumb drive to Iranian centrifuges, with the intention of causing physical damage. Stuxnet was designed to exploit the vulnerabilities of **supervisory control and data acquisition** (**SCADA**) interfaces, which exist in industrial devices that have not been designed to be connected to the internet. Another relevant channel of diffusion is made up of wireless connections and connected devices inside the latest generation of vehicles. Even in 2015 it was possible to exploit the vulnerabilities of the car's connectivity system, which allowed attackers to interact with the vehicle's accelerator, the air conditioner, and potentially also with the brakes.

In the same way, the possibility of connecting heterogeneous devices to each other gives rise to the possible creation of IoT botnets, which can seriously compromise the security and confidentiality of people, taking advantage of not only televisions and IP cameras, but also baby monitors and household appliances. But perhaps the most disturbing aspect is the fact that many implantable healthcare devices can be compromised by exploiting IoT vulnerabilities. Not surprisingly, in January 2017, the USA's **Food and Drug Administration** (**FDA**) in a notice announced the possibility that radio frequency-enabled implantable devices (including pacemakers and defibrillators) may be subject to attacks that could compromise the confidentiality of information, which may endanger the safety of patients.

In the following section, we see how blockchain technology can help counter IoT security threats.

Solving IoT security issues with blockchain

The use of blockchain in the field of IoT allows us to solve problems related to access verification, confidentiality, and data integrity. It is possible to implement blockchain-based solutions to ensure not only that data is exclusively accessed by trusted devices and appliances, but that the data exchanged by IoT devices is not altered. Let's see how to use blockchain to protect IoT healthcare devices. In recent times, the use of healthcare devices connected via wireless networks has grown significantly. Among the most popular healthcare devices are heart rate monitors, blood pressure monitors, insulin pumps, and blood pressure monitors.

The data transferred from these devices could be intercepted by attackers by eavesdropping on wireless connections. In this way, as a result of the disclosure of sensitive medical data, not only would the confidentiality and privacy of patients be at risk, but also their safety. In fact, an attacker could alter the data in transit using data injection techniques. This way, an attacker would inject malicious commands and incorrect values with the intention of attacking the patient's safety. Just think, for example, of an insulin pump that increases the insulin dose in response to incorrect values of blood glucose levels. Even in the case of IoT, the solution could consist of implementing an appropriate smart contract that manages the interaction of IoT devices and sensors with medical data. The correct reading of the medical data referred to the patients would be mediated by the smart contract, whose functions can only be accessed by trusted appliances and authorized operators.

Any changes made to medical data would be immediately verifiable by authorized operators and devices. The smart contract would notify the interested parties (medical operators and even the patient) of the data received and the treatments to be authorized. Furthermore, only the identifiers associated with the events that have occurred could be stored within the blockchain, while no sensitive information would be stored directly within the blockchain. In this way, sensitive information on medical data would be stored securely on external databases (in off-chain mode) and medical data would be protected by encryption, in compliance with the HIPAA rules. The transactions stored in the blockchain would therefore attest that the data was successfully processed, and could also be used in the event of any legal disputes.

In the following section, we deal with the problems of blockchain's compliance with the EU's GDPR privacy law.

Reconciling blockchain with the GDPR

Without any claim to exhaustiveness, in this section we examine the main points of contrast and friction between blockchain technology and the European Union's **General Data Protection Regulation** (**GDPR**), which can make compliance with European privacy legislation particularly demanding. The GDPR came into force in May 2018, and introduces a series of fundamental rights to guarantee the correct processing of personal data relating to European citizens.

To protect these fundamental rights, a series of obligations (and penalties, in the event of non-fulfillment) are provided by the GDPR that fall on the subjects who assume the role of data controllers. Data controllers are all those subjects that can decide the purposes and means of personal data processing. From what we have said so far, some difficulties in the correct application of the GDPR rules to data processing in the blockchain are immediately evident.

In the following section, let's examine the main points of contrast between GDPR and blockchain.

Blockchain versus GDPR

The main points of contrast between GDPR and blockchain are attributable to two fundamental factors. First of all, the GDPR rules assume that it is always possible to identify one or more subjects who assume the role of data controller. As mentioned in the previous section, the obligations and penalties provided for by the GDPR fall on the data controllers. Now, in the case of blockchain, due to its distributed and decentralized nature, it is difficult to establish who exactly holds the role of data controller. Consequently, it is difficult to identify the subjects deemed responsible on the basis of the accountability principle introduced in Article 5 of the GDPR.

Secondly, the GDPR requires that personal data may be modified or even deleted, in the event that this proves necessary pursuant to Articles 16 (the right to rectification) and 17 (the right to be forgotten). The reason for contrast in this case is determined by the fact that blockchain makes changes to data (not to mention cancellations) extremely expensive in order to guarantee the fundamental requirement of data integrity. To concretely examine the consequences on compliance, we must analyze the fundamental concepts introduced by the GDPR.

In the following section, we begin our analysis, starting with personal data.

Personal data in the GDPR

The fundamental rule introduced by the GDPR regarding personal data is contained in Article 4, which defines personal data as any information relating to an identified or identifiable natural person (or data subject). An identifiable natural person is anyone who can be identified directly or indirectly on the basis of the processing of data referring to them. Therefore the name or surname, but also biometric evidence, or digital identifiers (such as geolocation, IP address, and so on) could be used to identify real identities.

It is therefore necessary to clarify that personal data is just that which refers to individuals, not to companies or organizations. Article 8 states that personal data must be processed for specified purposes and on the basis of the consent of the person concerned. With regard to the processing of personal data in a blockchain, various difficulties arise in terms of compliance with the GDPR.

First, it is necessary to clarify whether the public keys used as identifiers (addresses) of a blockchain's users should also be considered personal data. But it remains uncertain how to obtain the express and informed consent to the data processing by the data subject. Furthermore, the consent must relate to the specific categories of data being processed. In fact, the GDPR provides that consent can only be considered informed if the data subject is aware of the purposes of the processing and can easily verify the identity of the data controller.

Furthermore, the demonstration that the informed consent to the processing of data has been legally obtained by the data subject falls on the data controller. Finally, based on Article 6, the data subject must be granted the right to withdraw consent.

In the following section, we will deal with the problem of public keys as personal data.

Public keys as personal data

Within a blockchain, each user is identified by means of their associated public key. This public key assumes a role analogous to bank account numbers in identifying the beneficiaries of transactions. The use of public keys as user identifiers allows the pseudo-anonymization of user identities, as we saw in the *Public keys as identities* section of `Chapter 8`, *Exploiting Blockchain as an Attack Vector*. In other words, using only public keys as identifiers, users can hide their identity, in the absence of other information available outside the blockchain, that traces the transactions to specific identities.

The pseudo-anonymization procedure used by blockchain seems to be in line with the provisions of Article 26 of the GDPR, which establishes the possibility of manipulating personal data by removing the reasonable likelihood of identifying a data subject. In reality, the use of public keys does not permit an adequate level of pseudo-anonymization. In fact, it is always possible to trace the real identity of the data subject identified by the public key by collecting additional information freely available on the web or by exploiting other public sources.

In light of this, therefore, even public keys can represent personal data, in the same way as, for example, IP addresses. According to the Working Party, which constitutes the advisory body with the task of providing interpretations of the GDPR, in the event that the public key is used to identify a data subject, it must always be considered personal data.

 In order to ensure effective data anonymization, it may therefore be useful to introduce the practice of using one-time public keys.

However, the enforcement of security practices is mainly achievable in the context of permissioned/private blockchains, rather than in public/permissionless blockchains, taking advantage of the governance mechanisms made available by the former type of network.

In the following section, we'll assess who holds the data controller role in a blockchain.

Assessing the data controller role in a blockchain

One of the main roles introduced by the GDPR is the data controller, which is discussed in Article 4. The data controller is the subject, a natural or legal person, that establishes the purposes and means used for the processing of personal data. It is the subject on which the obligations and penalties fall, in the event of non-fulfillment required by the GDPR, in compliance with the principle of accountability.

Pursuant to Article 26 of the GDPR, it is possible that there is more than one data controller, if more than one person together decide the purposes and means of the data processing. In this case, we should speak more properly of joint controllers. Based on the previous definitions, we understand the difficulties in determining which subjects can play the role of data controller or joint controllers in the blockchain. Even in the case of permissioned blockchains and DLTs, it is often not clear how to distinguish which subjects decide the means and purposes of the data processing carried out through the blockchain.

By analogy, we could refer to what already happens in the context of cloud computing. In this case, cloud providers are clearly considered data controllers, as they are the ones who choose which hardware and software platforms to use for data processing. In the case of the blockchain, due to its nature of a distributed architecture designed to be managed by several different organizations, there could be many actors who determine the choice of the method of data processing. In general, even in the case of permissioned/private blockchains and DLTs, often there is not a single legal entity that decides which hardware and software tools to use.

On the contrary, the choice of the means to be used is often left to the decision-making autonomy of the individual actors of the network. Just think, for example, of the choices made by miners on which hardware to use when mining blocks. Similar considerations can be drawn regarding the purposes of data processing. In the case of private/permissioned DLTs, it is possible to identify a specific legal entity (such as the consortium of companies) that establishes the purposes of data processing, and which therefore assumes the role of data controller.

However, it cannot be excluded that other actors may also play the role of joint controllers, and consequently, the obligations and responsibilities introduced by the GDPR do not fall only on a single legal entity. It is therefore necessary to investigate case by case and constantly monitor the real situation, in order to correctly establish the roles covered by the different actors.

In the following section, we will examine one of the main obligations introduced by the GDPR that falls on the data controller, and the application of which remains highly controversial within blockchain: the right to be forgotten.

Complying with the right to be forgotten

One of the most controversial rules introduced by the GDPR is **the right to be forgotten**. Pursuant to Article 17, data subjects must be granted the right to obtain the erasure of their personal data from the data controller.

The request for the erasure of personal data must be fulfilled promptly and without delay by the data controller in the following cases:

- The personal data is no longer necessary to achieve the original purposes.
- The data subjects withdraw their consent to data processing, according to Article 6 or Article 9.
- The personal data has been unlawfully processed by the data controller.

Furthermore, the data controller may be required to delete personal data as a result of a legal obligation. There are some exceptions to the exercise of the right to be forgotten by the data subject. This could happen when the right of freedom of expression and information must be respected, or for reasons of public interest in the area of public health, or for the exercise or defense of legal claims.

The difficulty of concrete application of the right to be forgotten in the cyberspace, in general, has been stressed by many critics. In the specific case of blockchain technology, compliance with this right is made even more difficult by the fact that this technology was designed specifically to make unilateral modification or deletion of data stored within the blockchain extremely complicated. The data integrity requirement is also considered a prerequisite for achieving trust in the network.

From a practical point of view, complying with the right to be forgotten in a blockchain that makes use of the **Proof of Work** (**PoW**) consensus mechanism would imply that the majority of the network nodes should do the following:

- Check the legitimacy of each transaction affected by the data erasure.

- Unbuild the entire blockchain.
- Rebuild the blockchain without the erased transactions.

The difficulty of implementing of the right to be forgotten is not only technical, however: there may also be network governance issues that make it difficult to force all nodes to update their local copy of the blockchain, as could happen in the case of public/permissionless blockchains. These issues have even been recognized by some data protection authorities, such as the French CNIL.

Therefore, some possible alternatives have been identified to raw data erasure, which we will discuss in the following section.

Possible alternatives to data erasure on blockchains

The aforementioned CNIL suggested deleting the private key corresponding to the public key used to encrypt the data to be deleted. In this way, the data to be deleted would remain inaccessible, even without having been physically erased. Other solutions refer to the adoption of blockchains specifically designed to allow the deletion of data through the use of chameleon hashes or pruning procedures, as in the case of the **functionality-preserving local erasure (FPLE)** approach introduced in `Chapter 8`, *Exploiting Blockchain as an Attack Vector*. However, it should be stressed that the difficulty of guaranteeing the right to be forgotten can be made impractical due to the lack of adequate coordination mechanisms between the different actors participating in the blockchain.

In the following section, we will conclude our analysis of the compatibility of blockchain technology with the GDPR regulation.

Assessing blockchain compatibility with the GDPR

Some final considerations are necessary at the end of our analysis of the compatibility between blockchain technology and the rules provided by the GDPR. It would be tempting to conclude that, due to the structural features offered by blockchain, this technology is substantially incompatible with the regulatory framework of the GDPR. In fact, it should be emphasized once again that blockchain does not constitute a single homogeneous technology, but rather a class of different implementations. Therefore, to draw a conclusive judgment on the compatibility or otherwise of a class of heterogeneous technologies with the GDPR is misleading.

Instead, it is necessary to carefully analyze the individual concrete implementations, and therefore to verify case by case the compatibility of the specific implementations with the rules provided by the GDPR. A general conclusion is, however, possible regarding which type of blockchain may be made more respectful of the rules of the GDPR. There is no doubt that private/permissioned blockchains can be more easily made compatible with the GDPR rules than public/permissionless blockchains.

This is possible because in permissioned networks, the various actors are known in advance, and the contractual ties that bind them together are just as well known, as are the aims and purposes that they intend to pursue with the introduction of the blockchain. Furthermore, permissioned blockchains provide for the enforcement of specific governance rules that allow the attribution of clear responsibilities in terms of compliance with the GDPR to specifically identified subjects.

These features allow greater control over the purposes and methods of data processing, as well as restricting access to data to authorized operators, in compliance with the rules introduced by the GDPR, which is instead difficult to achieve with public/permissionless blockchains.

Summary

In this chapter, we have examined the most delicate aspects regarding compliance with privacy requirements in the context of the processing of sensitive data carried out through blockchain. We have dealt with various aspects regarding the use of blockchain in the healthcare sector, and the critical issues associated with the growing diffusion of IoT technologies adopted in managing medical data. We also analyzed the possible advantages offered by the adoption of the blockchain to mitigate the vulnerabilities of IoT devices. Finally, we dealt with compliance issues with the GDPR, analyzing the main aspects of the EU legislation that are difficult to apply within the blockchain.

Congratulations! You have come to the end of a demanding path that has led you to greater awareness of securing blockchain. We hope you enjoyed your reading!

Other Books You May Enjoy

If you enjoyed this book, you may be interested in these other books by Packt:

Blockchain Development for Finance Projects

Ishan Roy

ISBN: 978-1-83882-909-4

Learn how to clean your data and ready it for analysis

- Design and implement blockchain solutions in a BFSI organization
- Explore common architectures and implementation models for enterprise blockchain
- Design blockchain wallets for multi-purpose applications using Ethereum
- Build secure and fast decentralized trading ecosystems with Blockchain
- Implement smart contracts to build secure process workflows in Ethereum and Hyperledger Fabric
- Use the Stellar platform to build KYC and AML-compliant remittance workflows
- Map complex business workflows and automate backend processes in a blockchain architecture

Hands-On Blockchain with Hyperledger
Nitin Gaur, Luc Desrosiers, Et al

ISBN: 978-1-78899-452-1

- Discover why blockchain is a game changer in the technology landscape
- Set up blockchain networks using basic Hyperledger Fabric deployment
- Understand the considerations for creating decentralized applications
- Learn to integrate business networks with existing systems
- Write Smart Contracts quickly with Hyperledger Composer
- Design transaction model and chaincode with Golang
- Deploy Composer REST Gateway to access the Composer transactions
- Maintain, monitor, and govern your blockchain solutions

Leave a review - let other readers know what you think

Please share your thoughts on this book with others by leaving a review on the site that you bought it from. If you purchased the book from Amazon, please leave us an honest review on this book's Amazon page. This is vital so that other potential readers can see and use your unbiased opinion to make purchasing decisions, we can understand what our customers think about our products, and our authors can see your feedback on the title that they have worked with Packt to create. It will only take a few minutes of your time, but is valuable to other potential customers, our authors, and Packt. Thank you!

Index

www.ingramcontent.com/pod-product-compliance
Lightning Source LLC
LaVergne TN
LVHW081522050326
832903LV00025B/1586